centre for educational research and innovation

DISABLED YOUTH:
FROM SCHOOL TO WORK

ORGANISATION FOR ECONOMIC CO-OPERATION AND DEVELOPMENT

Pursuant to Article 1 of the Convention signed in Paris on 14th December 1960, and which came into force on 30th September 1961, the Organisation for Economic Co-operation and Development (OECD) shall promote policies designed:

— to achieve the highest sustainable economic growth and employment and a rising standard of living in Member countries, while maintaining financial stability, and thus to contribute to the development of the world economy;
— to contribute to sound economic expansion in Member as well as non-member countries in the process of economic development; and
— to contribute to the expansion of world trade on a multilateral, non-discriminatory basis in accordance with international obligations.

The original Member countries of the OECD are Austria, Belgium, Canada, Denmark, France, Germany, Greece, Iceland, Ireland, Italy, Luxembourg, the Netherlands, Norway, Portugal, Spain, Sweden, Switzerland, Turkey, the United Kingdom and the United States. The following countries became Members subsequently through accession at the dates indicated hereafter: Japan (28th April 1964), Finland (28th January 1969), Australia (7th June 1971) and New Zealand (29th May 1973). The Commission of the European Communities takes part in the work of the OECD (Article 13 of the OECD Convention). Yugoslavia takes part in some of the work of the OECD (agreement of 28th October 1961).

The Centre for Educational Research and Innovation was created in June 1968 by the Council of the Organisation for Economic Co-operation and Development.
The main objectives of the Centre are as follows:

– *to promote and support the development of research activities in education and undertake such research activities where appropriate;*
– *to promote and support pilot experiments with a view to introducing and testing innovations in the educational system;*
– *to promote the development of co-operation between Member countries in the field of educational research and innovation.*

The Centre functions within the Organisation for Economic Co-operation and Development in accordance with the decisions of the Council of the Organisation, under the authority of the Secretary-General. It is supervised by a Governing Board composed of one national expert in its field of competence from each of the countries participating in its programme of work.

Publié en français sous le titre :

LES JEUNES HANDICAPÉS :
DE L'ÉCOLE A LA VIE ACTIVE

© OECD, 1991
Applications for permission to reproduce or translate
all or part of this publication should be made to:
Head of Publications Service, OECD
2, rue André-Pascal, 75775 PARIS CEDEX 16, France

The Centre for Educational Research and Innovation (CERI) of the Organisation for Economic Co-operation and Development (OECD) launched a programme of activities in 1978 on the themes of integration and transition to adult and working life for young people who are handicapped. This programme was widely supported by Member countries.

From 1982 to 1986 a programme of activities on the theme of transition from school to adult and working life was carried out. This was made possible by generous financial assistance from the United States Office of Special Education and Rehabilitation. The programme resulted in a number of reports including *Young People with Handicaps - The Road to Adulthood* published in 1986.

During 1986 a study was undertaken of national policies for children and young people who are handicapped, with the co-operation of the authorities in Australia, France and Sweden. At the end of the study a high-level conference was held in Paris in December 1986 resulting in a further series of reports.

The programme of activities concerned with young people with disabilities is now drawing to a close with a series of detailed studies of particular aspects of transition. One of these activities is devoted to the management of transition.

Among the outstanding issues to be highlighted in the transition programme was the question of how to achieve continuity and provide a recognisable point of reference for young people and their families during the transition phase. This was viewed from a number of different standpoints including:

a) The information and support necessary to enable young people, and their families, to manage their own transition through the maze of different government departments and agency responsibilities;

b) Effective means of providing continuity of support as individuals move from education through training to work and adult life;

c) The co-ordination of different education, health, social welfare and employment policies and services during adolescence towards agreed objectives for adult status and the maximum autonomy.

The more detailed study of the management of transition involved three elements. A review of the outcomes of the transition programme, the commissioning of a series of studies of specific arrangements in Member countries identified by the review and a small working seminar in Denmark in November 1988. The seminar was arranged with the active co-operation of the Danish authorities.

This report, concerned with "case management", covers all the work done on this aspect of transition including the findings of the seminar. It is in three parts.

Part I   Describes the main outcomes and issues to emerge from the transition programme and the context for the particular study of "case management";

Part II   Consists of the commissioned studies of transition management;

Part III   Draws conclusions about effective means to help individuals and their families to manage their own transition.

This report has been prepared by consultants and the Secretariat. The views expressed in Part II are those of the authors of the papers. The views expressed elsewhere, as an outcome of the study, do not commit the Organisation or the national authorities concerned.

Also available

DISABLED YOUTH: THE RIGHT TO ADULT STATUS (1988)
(96 88 02 1) ISBN 92-64-13132-9   FF55   £6.50   US$12.50   DM24

YOUNG PEOPLE WITH HANDICAPS: THE ROAD TO ADULTHOOD (1986)
(96 87 01 1) ISBN 92-64-12903-0   FF65   £6.50   US$13.00   DM29

THE INTEGRATION OF THE HANDICAPPED IN SECONDARY SCHOOLS: FIVE CASE STUDIES (1985)
(96 85 03 1) ISBN 92-64-12774-7   FF80   £8.00   US$16.00   DM36

HANDICAPPED YOUTH AT WORK: PERSONAL EXPERIENCES OF SCHOOL–LEAVERS (1985)
(96 85 02 1) ISBN 92-64-12708-9   FF55   £5.50   US$11.00   DM25

Prices charged at the OECD Bookshop.
The OECD CATALOGUE OF PUBLICATIONS and supplements will be sent free of charge on request addressed either to OECD Publications Service,
2, rue André–Pascal, 75775 PARIS CEDEX 16,
or to the OECD Distributor in your country

TABLE OF CONTENTS

Part I

A FRAMEWORK FOR TRANSITION

The Background 9
Criteria for Evaluating Transitional Arrangements 11
The Purposes of the Study 12

Part II

STUDIES OF TRANSITION IN SELECTED COUNTRIES

The *Kurator* System in Denmark 17
by Gia Boyd Kjellen

The Liaison Officer in Sweden 25
by Eje Hultkvist

Accompanying Services in France: Rehabilitation Follow-up Teams 33
by Thibault Lambert

Developing Individual Service Plans for People with Severe Disabilities, Manchester, United Kingdom 39
by Mick Molloy

Case Management in the United States 49
by Ruth Luckasson

Part III

CONCLUSIONS

Essential Elements in Managing Transition 67

Part I

A FRAMEWORK FOR TRANSITION

THE BACKGROUND

Adulthood

One of the first questions to ask about transition is transition to what? It is far from certain that a young person with a disability will be expected to become an adult or will be treated as one. The question of how adult status is or is not achieved was an important element in the transition project.

The broad conclusion was reached that "adulthood" is a less than precise description of a legal and social status and of a range of individual, social and economic choices. It may be defined differently in different countries and cultures but there are common features. "Coming of age" can be observed in four main areas of life:

a) Personal autonomy and independence;
b) Productive activity;
c) Social interaction, community participation, recreational and leisure activities;
d) Roles within the family.

One of the problems in most modern developed societies is that each of these areas of life tends to be dealt with separately by a different department or agency.

What is needed is a conceptual framework for transition which encompasses all aspects of the move through adolescence to adulthood. Within this framework there needs to be a clear statement of objectives in behavioural terms. If these objectives could be agreed by all agencies, by professionals, by parents and above all by the young people themselves, there might be a more concerted effort to develop coherent approaches to the process of transition and less confusion in areas of responsibility.

Phases of Transition

The OECD/CERI study recognised three inter-related phases of the transition process, namely:

a) The final years of schooling;
b) Further education and vocational preparation; and
c) Entry into work and adult life.

These phases will cover varying time scales in Member countries but they each have different characteristics. There is a need to recognise their inter-relationships.

The Concept of Handicap

The time of transition reveals confusion in the use of the term handicap (this issue is discussed more fully in Educational Monograph No. 1, OECD/CERI, 1987). Traditionally it has been a label attached to individual deficits. Two things have become increasingly clear, namely, that it is important to distinguish between a disability and its handicapping effects, and that for the same disability these effects vary from person to person and from situation to situation.

It follows from this situational and individual definition of handicap that to categorise people by a single criterion, such as a specific disability, is wrong. It leads to stereotyping, to inappropriate expectations and to a lack of planning for individual needs.

During the transition phase, education, social service, health and employment agencies may use different criteria to define who is handicapped. Some definitions are based on the help needed for the individual to be as independent as possible and others are based on the assumption that the individual remains totally dependent. These differences reflect attitudes which may be crucial to individual development during adolescence.

What modern methods and technology have achieved is a lessening of the handicapping effects of many disabilities with a consequent raising of expectations. We should no longer talk about "a handicapped person" but about "a person who is handicapped". This is not just a semantic quibble. It represents a significant change and a recognition that it is attitudes, situations and administrative decisions which determine whether disabilities are more or less handicapping.

Assessment

The process of assessment is potentially handicapping. In practice an individual's behaviour, achievement and response to education may be very potent determinants of what is offered on leaving school. Being in a special group may limit what is expected and offered. But the skills and knowledge expected in school may bear little relationship to those expected in most living and working situations.

The purpose of an assessment and the evidence on which it is based are important considerations. If the purpose is to categorise, then the result may lead to stereotyping and low expectation. If the evidence is school performance, then the result may be relevant to further education but not to employment and independent living. Capacities for employment and for independent living should not be assessed without observing experience in those situations. Assessment should lead to a plan for the individual and not be a prediction simply based on past performance.

Major Problems of Transition

These have been described in detail in the OECD/CERI publication *Young People with Handicaps - The Road to Adulthood, op.cit.* Major issues may be summarised briefly as follows:

Different Starting Points. At the end of the school period individuals may be in regular classes, special classes, special schools, hospitals and residential institutions. They may leave schools at different ages. A major question is how far the situation and the age from which transition starts result in preconceived ideas which limit the range of opportunities that is offered to the individual.

Continuity. In each of the three phases already described, different agencies and professions have different objectives and may attempt to cover different curricula. It is becoming increasingly important to develop a continuity of concern, curriculum and objectives.

Consistency. Individuals and their families face inconsistent demands and attitudes. One agency may be giving support to develop employment skills while another may be awarding pensions and benefits on the basis of the individual's incompetence. Is it in the individual's best interests to remain dependent? There needs to be some consistency in expectations from one agency to another.

Time Scale. There is no doubt from international experience that extended education and training, particularly for young people with severe disabilities, pays off in terms of employment and independence. In the United States or Sweden an individual would normally remain in high school until at least 18 and then have at least between two and four years vocational preparation. Compare this with the one or two years offered after the age of 16 in other countries. Adult competence is often expected from those at the greatest disadvantage many years before it is expected of others whose education is extended.

Co-ordination. The young person with a disability might well ask whether health, education and social services know what each other are doing and whether they work with voluntary organisations. There is a need for a great deal more local co-ordination at least to the point of agreeing on common objectives.

Parents and Transition. It is during the transition phase that parents of young people with disabilities may become particularly concerned about their children's future and, without help, may inhibit progress towards adulthood. Professionals need to work with them over time to develop an idea of the adult life that is possible. Information is not enough. A new three-way relationship needs to be formed between parents, professionals and the young person concerned.

Self-presentation and Advocacy. We need to move away from the "eternal childhood" model of disability towards a more positive view of adult status. New relationships will not be possible unless those with disabilities are enabled to express their views and manage their affairs.

Categorical or Individual Thinking. We have had a tradition of people being labeled according to category of handicap and then receiving a package of services, whether they need them or not. How far can we individualise service delivery? How far do we expect individuals to achieve an adult status where they manage their own resources and select the services they need? By labeling someone as disabled do we automatically assume that they must be dependent on professionals and agencies?

CRITERIA FOR EVALUATING TRANSITIONAL ARRANGEMENTS

It is possible to begin to look at the transition phase as a whole and to ask questions about it. These questions can be a form of evaluation and might include:
1. What are the objectives of assessment at the end of schooling? Are they to categorise or to develop an individual plan?
2. What is the balance of the curriculum in the final school years and in further education? What is the respective weight given to academic, social, vocational and life skills objectives?

3. What information is available to young people and their families about the range of transition facilities and services available to them?
4. What continuity of concern, curriculum and objectives is there between the three phases of transition?
5. How are parents and families involved in planning and supporting their child's transition?
6. How far do transitional arrangements encourage the development of independence, autonomy and self-advocacy?
7. Do professional practices and areas of responsibility affect the development of effective transitional arrangements?
8. What financial arrangements support an individual and his or her family during transition? How far do these arrangements inhibit or facilitate autonomy and adult status?
9. When we aim for community provision and participation, how do we define community?

These questions add up to a review of how transition is managed. It is this management aspect of the process which was the main objective of the study.

THE PURPOSES OF THE STUDY

The period of transition from school to adult and working life for young people who are disabled is often a bewildering array of services and areas of professional responsibility. From a relatively simple situation, where the school is a natural focus for professional co-operation, individuals and families move to an often uncharted territory where there are few clear signposts and where different service criteria and objectives may not be compatible.

One of the major issues to emerge from the OECD/CERI transition project was the need to look in more detail at the ways in which transition can be managed more successfully. The term "case management" has been used to summarise the issue but it is a shorthand requiring explanation.

The different contexts in Member countries and regions within them, together with their cultural values and social policies for young people, are a powerful influence on the transition process and on the adult status it is possible for those with disabilities to achieve. However, given that all individuals have to make some form of transition, there are common concerns about how this is best managed.

The purpose of the study was to discuss these common concerns in detail, to examine practices which appear to be effective in facilitating a successful transition and to look at ways in which important features of those practices might be incorporated into professional practices in other countries.

Study Themes

There are three broad themes for the study:
a) The development of coherent transition plans for individuals during a phase when different agencies, with different responsibilities, may not be working towards the same objectives;

b) The achievement of a proper balance between the management of their own transition by individuals and its management by professionals;
c) The identification of professional activities and services that are effective in facilitating the transition of individuals and in helping their families to accord adult status.

Outstanding Issues

The study was intended to address a number of specific issues. The focus was on the individual and his or her family and the ways in which agencies and services contribute to transition. Among topics for discussion were:

a) Are there agreed objectives for transition to which departments and agencies work?
b) In what ways is information made available to individuals and their families to enable them to plan transition?
c) To whom can individuals and their families turn for help during transition?
d) Are plans for transition made individually or are there stereotyped and limited expectations and opportunities linked with categories of handicap?
e) What continuity exists over the move from school to work and independent living, and who provides that continuity?
f) How are individuals prepared for managing their own transition?
g) What kinds of person are seen as helpful in assisting transition, what do they do and how should they be trained?
h) Among the range of role options — key worker, facilitator, case manager, progress chaser, guide, counsellor — which seems to be the most appropriate within the multi-agency context of transition?

Part II

STUDIES OF TRANSITION IN SELECTED COUNTRIES

THE *KURATOR* SYSTEM IN DENMARK

by
Gia Boyd Kjellen

Introduction

One of the particular concerns to emerge from the OECD/CERI transition study was the ways in which young people and their families get information, guidance and counselling during this important phase in their lives. Different options and agency responsibilities present a complex challenge to case management and guidance services.

A unique approach, identified in Denmark, was the *Kurator* system. In preparation for a specific study of case management during transition it was decided to study the *Kurator* system in more detail. This abridged report is based on a study visit during one week in May 1987.

The Programme of the Visit

Two days were spent in discussions and visits in Copenhagen setting the work of *Kurators* within the context of special educational developments. Three days were spent looking at the work of *Kurators* in the Odense area. During this period visits were paid to schools and other facilities and discussions took place with young people and their parents.

The Education System

A comprehensive school system, from the 1st to the 10th grade, was established by the Education *(Folkeskole)* Act of 1975. The Act lays down the fundamental principles that everyone, regardless of gender, social origins, geographical origins and physical or mental disabilities, shall have the same access to education and training.

There is no division of compulsory education into stages and all pupils attend the same school from the pre-school stage up to the 10th grade. However, children attending *Folkeskolen* can finish their last two years in a continuation school *(Efterskole)* if they wish. Some of the continuation schools are specially designed for disabled pupils and combine teaching and practical work.

If pupils choose an academically-oriented education after completing the *Folkeskole* course, they can aim for either courses in *Gymnasia,* or courses leading to Higher Preparatory Examination. The latter is an alternative way of gaining qualifications for higher and further education.

Students choosing a vocationally-oriented education can either apply for apprenticeship training (2-4 years) or a basic vocational education (EFG).

Another element in the system are youth schools run by municipalities for young people between 14 and 18. These provide a wide range of courses to enable less skilled young people to become more employable.

Legislation

Brief descriptions of legislation relevant to children and young people who have disabilities or significant difficulties are set out below:

Education Department Order on Special Education in the Folkeskole - 1978. This order, implemented in 1980, transferred responsibilities for the education of pupils with disabilities from the Ministry of Social Affairs to the Ministry of Education. Municipalities and counties had to assume responsibility for provision and to finance it with the assistance of block grants from the government.

Paragraph 19 of the order sets out the respective responsibilities of counties and municipalities for provision and services. It is the responsibility of:

a) Counties (Para 19.2) to educate pupils with severe *(vidtgaende)* disabilities. This is often referred to as Paragraph 19.2 education.
b) Municipalities (Para. 19.1) to educate other pupils with disabilities and special educational needs.

Departmental Order under the Social Security Act 1976 amended 1979. This lays down procedures for *Kurators* to inform Social Service Departments about pupils in special classes. There is no duty to inform social services, although in some municipalities it is an agreed procedure, but to do so enables pupils to get financial assistance, particularly if they attend a continuation school. Assistance is based on parental income.

Paragraph 42 Social Security Act 1976. This paragraph deals with financial assistance for vocational rehabilitation or further education after a young person reaches the age of 18. The *Kurator* helps pupils to apply for assistance. Municipal authorities decide what assistance an individual is entitled to and for what period. This assistance is not dependent on parental income but in some cases may be given as a loan.

Ministry of Education Departmental Order 1988 (draft). This order, which has been circulated for comment, will set out the duties of school psychologists with respect to young people leaving school and the assistance *Kurators* can give to students in entering further education and obtaining work.

Law on Youth Guidance. This legislation, implemented in 1981, ensures that all young people are given guidance about education and training until they reach the age of 19.

The Special Education System

Special education in Denmark has a long history. The Royal Institute for the Deaf was opened in 1807 and compulsory attendance introduced in 1871. The Royal Institute for the Blind opened in 1811 and compulsory school attendance for the blind was introduced in 1926. The first school for children with psychological and learning disorders was opened in 1855 and attendance was made compulsory in 1959. All these schools were privately financed with a contribution from the State until 1934 when the State assumed responsibility for running the schools.

The first municipal classes for what were then called backward children, were started in 1900. Classes for children with reading difficulties were started in 1955 and for children with motor disabilities in 1961. Finally, classes for psychotic children were started in 1967.

From the 1950s municipalities had responsibilities to meet special educational needs but children with severe disabilities were sent to state schools. In 1980 counties and municipalities took over responsibility for these schools. At the same time *Folkeskolen* had to provide support for pupils whose development required it and pupils with severe disabilities were assured of eleven years schooling.

The changes brought about by the 1980 Act are based on the principles of normalization, decentralisation and integration. All disabled children have the same right to education as others. Normalization is seen as a challenge to society to adapt rather than a demand on the individual to adapt to society.

Who Receives Special Education

Pupils with learning difficulties, for which special education is considered necessary, fall into four main groups:
- a) Pupils with specific physical and sensory disabilities, e.g. of vision, hearing and motor function;
- b) Pupils with general difficulties in learning, e.g. slow learners, children with intellectual disabilities and with psychological developmental disorders;
- c) Pupils with social adjustment difficulties, e.g. children with behaviour difficulties, social and emotional disorders and psychological disorders;
- d) Pupils with specific difficulties, e.g. retarded readers and children with dyslexia.

In the academic year 1983/84 special education took up 16 per cent of the total hours of both regular and special education in *Folkeskolen*.

The Structure of the *Kurator* System

The branch of the Ministry of Education responsible for special education is the Directorate of *Folkeskole* and Teacher Training. Within the Special Education Section there is a part-time *Kurator* advisor. The advisor acts as a link between the Ministry and *Kurators* in the field. This is a position held by a working *Kurator* who gives three days a week to the Ministry and works two days a week in the municipality in which he or she is employed. The part-time advisory post is an appointment which can be held for up to seven years.

A *Kurator* is always a *Folkeskole* teacher qualified to teach in grades 1 to 10. Being a *Kurator* is not a separate career. There is no formal training but most *Kurators* have taken additional courses in guidance and special education since qualification. A *Kurator* post within schools is one for which experienced teachers apply and those appointed are teachers who know their school and neighbourhood well.

At present there are 140 *Kurators*, 110 of whom are school counsellors and 30 combine being a *Kurator* with being a guidance teacher.

Each municipality works out its own plan for the work of *Kurators*. If schools are small they may share the same guidance team and small municipalities may also share guidance teams. There is no set work plan for Kurators, who work closely with class teachers, and they develop their own pattern of work within the guidance team.

The Guidance Team

There is a counselling system in all schools maintained by a team which includes the school psychologist, a guidance teacher, a youth advisor and may include a *Kurator*. It is obligatory to employ a guidance teacher but not a *Kurator*.

Guidance Teachers: The 1975 Education Act states that there must be a guidance teacher in every school. His duties are to offer guidance to all pupils in grades 7 to 10 about their choice of subjects, about opportunities for further education and about employment possibilities. He arranges work experience and brings in speakers from training institutions and the world of work as part of a guidance programme. A concrete work plan is laid down in a ministry circular for guidance teachers.

Youth Advisors: Legislation, passed in 1981, states that all young people living in a municipality should have access to an advisor concerned with training and work possibilities for up to two years after leaving school or at least up to the age of 19. The aim of guidance is to ease transition from school to further education and work. Guidance sessions should take place twice a year.

Kurator: The third member of the team is the *Kurator* who is an advisor and guide for pupils with learning difficulties who attend special classes. The extent of pupils' disabilities and their severity in these classes varies from area to area. Some *Kurators* may also help children with disabilities integrated into regular classes.

Pupils have a right to a *Kurator* while still at school. Once they leave, ex-pupils have to contact the *Kurator* if they want continued help. The *Kurator* has no duty to follow them up.

Many *Kurators* also work as youth advisors and give disabled pupils the same services as youth advisors including the twice-yearly meeting and the statutory obligation to follow their progress after leaving school. *Kurators* who also work as youth advisors get additional hours to work with disabled young people.

Co-ordination

Local councils should co-cordinate all the various guidance arrangements in the municipality for young people under 25. They should also produce a youth team consisting of representatives of the various guidance systems including school and youth advisors, social services and the employment agency. In some municipalities *Kurators* will be included in the team but this is something decided by each local authority.

The Work of a *Kurator*

The *Kurator* could be described as a transition specialist. He has specialised knowledge of community relations, vocational placement and liaison with other agencies. Guidance during transition is done in co-operation with disabled students, their parents and their teachers. It is an informal process not regulated by legislative rules which aims to develop and facilitate an individual plan for each student.

The guidance *Kurators* can give covers work, training, leisure time use, family relationships and the economics of family living. The counselling is general and not psychological. If more intensive personal counselling is needed this will be done by psychological services or other agencies.

A *Kurator* is employed by a local authority with a minimum of 2 000 pupils in municipal schools. He is allowed a reduction in his teaching for guidance and liaison work according to the school population. If the number of pupils is between 2 000 and 2 500 there is a reduction of four hours; from 2 501 to 3 000 pupils there is a reduction of five hours and thereafter a reduction of one additional hour for each 1 000 pupils. In larger municipalities a *Kurator* will work in a district with at least 5 000 pupils.

Various job descriptions for *Kurators* exist because each local authority can work out its own. The Danish Union of Teachers has one which is as follows. *The Kurator:*

- a) Carries out his work under the responsibility of the central leadership of the school. He is also an assistant to the main school psychologist;
- b) Gives advice on the conditions in the school, possibilities for training and jobs during the school years, and during the first years of transition, to pupils in special classes, pupils with general difficulties in learning, other retarded children and their parents. [Lately there is a tendency for the *Kurator* to follow many of these pupils up into their twenties];
- c) Works with class teachers, head teachers, the school guidance team, the school nurse, the school doctor and other health and social service agencies to build up a complete picture of the pupils concerned;
- d) Has the responsibility, where appropriate in co-operation with the class teacher and other guidance personnel, to see that pupils get guidance on training and employment opportunities;
- e) Has the responsibility for making contacts with employers about pupils needing special consideration. With the parents' permission, the *Kurator* is also able to make contact with employment agencies and employers to find jobs for pupils;
- f) Should be well informed about employment and social security legislation as well as conditions and wages. He should be aware of local conditions and take part in meetings about the development of transitional arrangements for the pupils who are his concern.

The local Education Committee in Odense produced a ten-point job description in 1976 which closely follows that of the Union.

A Working Week

In Odense, a town of 170 000 inhabitants, about 17 000 pupils from pre-school to 10th grade attend 42 *Folkeskoler*. In six of the schools there are special classes for pupils with general learning difficulties. In 1986/87 there were four *Kurators* to work with 285 pupils in these classes.

A typical working week, as observed in Odense, would start, say, on Monday morning with a two-hour period in the office at the school in which the *Kurator* is based. The four *Kurators* in Odense share six schools but have their own offices in a particular school. This two-hour period is an important one when parents, teachers and other people concerned with the pupil and the family can be sure to contact the *Kurator* after the weekend. The *Kurator* also makes sure that there is one other fixed time during the week, after school hours, when he can be reached by telephone.

Teaching in special classes or regular classes takes up most of the week. There is an obligatory two hours devoted to educational and vocational orientation but other teaching time might be in any subject with any grade.

The reduction in teaching hours, which the *Kurator* has, provides time to visit young people undergoing work experience or in work. New possible employers are sought and liaison maintained with a network of colleagues involved in the transition phase.

Continued contact with parents is an important part of the work and regular visits to home and meetings are held usually after school hours to enable both parents to be involved.

With Whom Do *Kurators* Work?

In practice *Kurators* work mainly with pupils with general learning difficulties who are in special classes. They may also work with pupils with other disabilities who are in regular classes.

The *Kurator* starts to give educational and vocational guidance in the 8th grade. The subject is taught for two hours each week from the 8th to the 10th grades. It is during these periods that the *Kurator* gets to know individuals and forms plans for continued education, work experience and work.

Some pupils may choose to attend courses lasting one or two years in continuation schools during the 9th or 10th grades. The *Kurator* is expected to have a wide knowledge of these schools and to help pupils choose schools and apply for places. *Kurators* will follow pupils when they attend such schools and assist in finding further training and perhaps work.

The *Kurator* may work with guidance teachers and class teachers to help individuals with disabilities in regular classes. Responsibility for their transition can be transferred to *Kurators* if there is a written request from the parents and the school to the guidance team. The *Kurator*'s work is to provide assistance with transitional arrangements similar to that given to pupils in special classes.

Managing Transition

Through the orientation lessons the pupil becomes aware of educational and vocational possibilities and gains some understanding of the world of work. There are two different aspects of work in the final school years, work experience and work placement. The former is experienced by all pupils and the latter is only possible for pupils in special classes during the 10th grade.

All pupils should have work experiences during the 8th, 9th and 10th grades. For pupils for whom the *Kurator* is responsible there is discussion about possibilities, consultation with the school doctor and discussion with and consent from parents. Pupils then go out for periods of work experience, in which they are not paid, during the school year and the *Kurator* pays visits to assess a pupil's response. Pupils can also attend short introductory courses at youth and technical schools.

Work placements are considered particularly important for young people with disabilities to give them confidence and enhance their chances of getting a job. During the 10th grade the *Kurator*'s pupils are helped to find work placements in a number of forms. For example, a pupil:

a) Might go to school from 8 a.m. to 11 a.m. each day and then to a work placement;
b) Might go to school three days a week and to work for two days or vice versa;
c) Might work full-time for a term and then return to school.

Working conditions and a reward is arranged for each pupil. This will be a payment from the employer which might be an agreed wage or might be made up of an employer's contribution supplemented by social service payments. Employers, parents and the young people themselves turn to the *Kurator* if any problems arise.

The *Kurator*'s Areas of Work and Networks

Through teaching and work with pupils, their families and a wide range of other professionals, the *Kurator* deals with the following aspects of his pupil's life:

a) *School circumstances.* Choice of subjects, vocational orientation, work experience and placement, continued education, educational grants, youth schools.
b) *Further education and training.* Continuation schools, evening schools, home economic schools, vocational schools, apprenticeships, basic vocational education and semi-skilled workers training schools.
c) *Working conditions.* Choice of career, applications, references, salaries and conditions, careers officers, employers, trade unions and legislation.
d) *Personal matters.* Disability, the home environment, economics, leisure time, accidents, military service, social security, public offices and services and social welfare.

Professional Training and Development

In 1953 a Commission on Youth recommended that "guides" should be attached to special education. They should help slow learners to get in contact with public and private institutions which might help them. Standard guidance for *Kurators* was introduced in 1968 because the importance of their work had been recognised and there was wide variation in working practices. The official status for *Kurators* was recognised in 1971 when they were established as school counsellors for the *Kurator* system.

There is as yet no standard training for *Kurators*. After teacher training and experience, many complete additional courses in guidance or special education. The Ministry of Education arranges a two-day conference each year for new *Kurators* and a conference to discuss their work. The National Association of *Kurators* — who are also members of the Teachers Union — has been established to promote and develop the work of *Kurators* and also holds a biennial conference. It has been decided to introduce a development course for 24 participants for two separate weeks in different terms during the academic year 1988/89.

Visits and Discussions

During the study, discussions took place with young people, parents, social workers and other professionals in schools and workshops.

Among the institutions visited were: *Folkeskolen,* a boarding school for adults, a sheltered workshop, a rehabilitation centre and a production high school (a school which combines practical and academic learning). These all play a part in transitional arrangements.

Comments

The work of *Kurators* in schools can give rise to tensions. A recent survey showed that some class teachers thought that the *Kurator* was interfering with the traditional role of the class teacher who, in Denmark, may stay with the same class for the whole of a child's school life. On the other hand *Kurators* thought that some class teachers had insufficient understanding of the problems of pupils with special educational needs.

Many post-school decisions about young people with disabilities are taken by social services. Parents thought that social workers had too many families to deal with and went for cheap solutions. Many parents thought they often had to fight for their children's rights.

A significant element in preparing for transition is the *Kurator*'s report to social services in the 9th or 10th grade. This is important in helping social workers plan post-school provision and financial support.

Interviews with young people illustrate the wide variety of help being given by *Kurators*. They appreciate the help given. Parents appreciate the informality of the system, some being happy with the contribution of *Kurators* and others feeling insufficiently involved in decision-making.

The Ministry of Education received the report of private consultants who reviewed the whole guidance system in 1987. Its findings are now being disseminated and considered and will influence the future work of *Kurators*. There is strong backing from the Ministry of Education for the *Kurator* system and wish to extend their work to all children receiving special education.

There are plans to double the number of *Kurators* but financial restraints make it difficult for the smaller municipalities to employ them. A programme of action to help slow learners is also being developed by the Ministry.

THE LIAISON OFFICER IN SWEDEN

by

Eje Hultkvist

Introduction

During the OECD/CERI Transition Project, the experimental work of the Liaison Officer was described in a Swedish position report in 1984. It was one of a number of initiatives to facilitate transition that have been studied in more detail for the Case Management Seminar. The report first describes the problems and then shows how the introduction of a liaison officer has helped to solve them.

While studying at the senior level of compulsory school, youngsters are expected to choose an education for a future job. To some, this is a task without great problems, but to most youngsters this task is filled with difficulties, difficulties which could make life exciting and stimulate new efforts. Some obstacles are, however, impossible to overcome. Admission requirements in the education system can mean that the desired education cannot be realised. Moreover, uncertainty in the labour market could make it very difficult to choose a profession.

Many youngsters have had to change their plans when the thought-of assignments have disappeared or been changed. Moreover, the short supply of jobs strikes extra hard on youngsters.

To youngsters with orthopedic handicaps, the choice of education or profession is more difficult than for other youngsters. The supply of jobs is, for them, even less.

Employment and residence are closely related. Many youngsters with orthopedic handicaps have to change their residential locality in order to find employment. The possibility to get a home of their own is, for many people, dependent on the access to personal assistance at many different times of the day.

Youngsters with orthopedic handicaps thus have even more substantial difficulties in carrying out their plans for the future. These problems are well known to those who work with these youngsters, and naturally, above all, to the youngsters themselves and to their parents.

Society has made, and is still making, considerable efforts to ameliorate the situation for people with orthopedic handicaps. In spite of these efforts, there are still great differences in the standard of living between the groups of people with orthopedic handicaps and the population as a whole.

In recent years, schools have taken increasing opportunities to admitting pupils with handicaps of various kinds on an integrated basis. The establishment of regional school consultants has undoubtedly meant a great deal in helping the individual school and its staff, through advice and assistance, to solve educational problems of various kinds. What is still lacking, however, is vocational guidance in greater depth and closer co-operation between schools and rehabilitation staff, as well as with the pupil and his family.

School Information

Young persons whom we talked to in the early part of this survey called for vocational guidance in which allowance was made for their situation as handicapped persons. They would have liked better information concerning educational opportunities which might be open to them both in upper secondary school and in other forms of education. These young persons felt that careers teachers and Vocational Guidance officers (SYO) today lacked experience of dealing with the problems of handicapped youngsters and were therefore unable to give them adequate assistance. They wanted more information about study routes which could be modified or adapted according to the situation of the individual handicapped pupil.

Today, only a small number of orthopedically handicapped youngsters are taking the vocational lines of upper secondary school. Many, on the other hand, have stated that they would have chosen studies of this kind if the programme had been adapted to suit their needs.

Most handicapped youngsters have less chance than their non-handicapped classmates of obtaining on-the-job training, which in turn means that they have less opportunity of acquiring work experience. To increase their opportunities in this respect, it is important to help them make use of the opportunities which PRYO (practical vocational orientation) can offer. Given careful planning, PRYO/PRAO (practical working life orientation, i.e. work experience) and extended PRYO or adjusted studies can be a great help. Some pupils may need extra experience of a particular occupational field before venturing into a long process of vocational education.

In connection with the transition to upper secondary school, handicapped youngsters need help in analysing their work situation and their assistance requirements. Work in upper secondary school is essentially different from compulsory school, and the individual pupil has to make plans for it in advance.

During their school career, moreover, handicapped youngsters must be helped to find feasible working methods for their subsequent employment or education.

All this means that the help required in upper secondary school can differ from that required in compulsory school. In order, therefore, to obtain a realistic picture of the work of upper secondary school, some of the young persons taking part in the project were given a trial week in the line of upper secondary school which they proposed taking.

Until now, notice of admission to upper secondary school has come late in the spring, leaving little time for practical planning. It is of course important for planning in connection with the transition to be completed before the transition actually takes place, for the pupil to be able to gain access to premises, for technical aids to be installed in advance, for a pupil's assistant to be engaged and so on. For pupils not spending a "PRYO" period at upper secondary school, an extra whole-day visit has been organised instead. In this way, each pupil, together with upper secondary staff, has been able to examine facilities and timetabling and discuss practical points. In many such cases the rehabilitation advisor has also taken part so as to recommend solutions.

Housing and Employment

Most disabled youngsters live with their parents while they are attending school. It has proved difficult for many of them to realise their ambition of a home of their own after leaving school. In cases where this has been possible, they have often had to change their residential locality, moving from a small community to a larger town or city. For many of them it has proved impossible to find both housing and employment in the same locality. These difficulties are often due to a lack of co-ordination between various agents. The shortage of modified flats is another major problem.

Housing and Independent Living

Housing and access to care services are carefully interconnected. Handicapped youngsters require services adapted to suit their need for contacts and social life — services which are available at the times when young people usually get together. A number of these young persons also require service round the clock if they are to be able to realise their aim of independent living.

Care of this kind can be provided for young persons who are able to obtain service accommodation, but it seems difficult to arrange for those having other forms of housing accommodation. Night-time home help services can seldom be arranged for those living in flats of their own away from their parents or for those continuing to live in the parental home.

As things now stand, most of the care received by handicapped youngsters is provided by their families. Only in exceptional cases have municipal authorities provided home help services for young persons living with their parents. The State, acting through the Care Services Board, has assumed responsibility for the care of young persons living away from home in order to study at folk high school or university.

Housing and access to care services are essential in order for young persons with severe orthopedic handicaps to be able to live independently. If the housing question is not adequately solved, there will be little prospect of employment and meaningful leisure.

The need for care must not be overlooked when helping young persons, during their school career, to plan for the future. It is important for the young persons themselves to analyse the assistance they require and the ways in which they prefer to receive it.

For some years now, jobs have been in short supply for all young persons. The *employment situation* for young persons with handicaps of various kinds has always been difficult. An increased supply of job opportunities does not always mean better prospects for handicapped youngsters.

These young persons therefore need special support and assistance in their efforts to find employment. This assistance must be offered at an early stage, which means that practical forms of collaboration between school and the various departments of the employment office must be devised while the pupils are still at the senior level of compulsory school. At present this very seldom happens. Consequently many young people today have had long waits between the end of their schooling and their first jobs.

Large numbers of them have confirmed that this waiting period has a devastating effect on their self-confidence, and it often intensifies their feeling of being handicapped and left out of things.

It is therefore important for young persons to explore every opportunity of finding a job. The supply of jobs which can be offered to handicapped youngsters today is extremely limited. A great deal of imagination is a good help in finding new jobs.

Wider opportunities of workplace adjustment and wage-subsidised employment of various kinds should make it possible for more young persons to be helped in finding employment. Over and above the possibilities already existing, new expedients should be tried, and this is in fact being done.

Leisure Time

Leisure activity opportunities of various kinds are important to all young persons, but unfortunately the leisure of young persons with orthopedic handicaps is often very constricted. Most of the activities of daily life are time consuming. Journeys to and from school often involve periods of waiting, and so on. Many handicapped youngsters, moreover, receive various forms of treatment which have to take place during leisure hours so as not to interfere too much with their school work.

But apart from the impact which all these things have on leisure hours, handicapped youngsters have limited opportunities of associating with other people of their own age. True, most of the young people interviewed said that they had friends, but for some of them having friends their own age is an unattainable dream and most of their leisure activities are shared with adults only.

Friends will seldom call to see a person who is unable to go and visit them. If a young person is prevented by an orthopedic handicap from going out independently and is dependent on help from adults, this reduces his contacts with friends of his own age. Transport assistance has been a solution where some young people are concerned, while in other cases parents and relatives have provided transport. Whatever the arrangements, however, spontaneous contacts with friends are always difficult to achieve so long as one is dependent on others for getting out.

An important part of the project has involved talking to young persons about the extent to which they believe they need help or support in order to make their leisure more rewarding. This can relate both to transport and to the establishment of contacts so as to join clubs or participate in other youth activities.

Co-operation is often needed between various public authorities in order for handicapped youngsters to participate in the various resources which the community has provided for them. At present, this is left entirely to the handicapped individual and his family.

The co-operation referred to here concerns measures within the individual municipality, but it can sometimes involve measures elsewhere. If a handicapped person wishes to move to a new locality in order to take up employment, this calls among other things for suitable housing, access to the requisite services and adequate transport assistance arrangements.

The Social Insurance Service and, often, vocational rehabilitation authorities also have to be contacted in connection with a change of residential locality, and various social welfare departments in both municipalities have to be notified to prevent grants and supportive measures from "drying up". The rehabilitation clinic in the new residential locality will require a referral, and so on. All these various things frequently involve the individual person in dealings with 10 or 15 different people (see figure). What is more, responsibilities within the various departments are often divided between several departments and officials. Unfortunately, responsibilities for co-operation and co-ordination within the individual authority are not always clearly defined.

These difficulties are widely attested by many handicapped youngsters and their parents. Many questions of concern to the individual have remained unsolved due to the inadequate co-ordination of practical measures.

Desirable as it may be, co-ordination of the activities of different authorities is definitely not a practical proposition. If the liaison officer is placed at the disposal of these young persons, each handicapped individual can be piloted through the bureaucracy. Through his experience of several cases of a similar nature, a liaison officer can establish routines making it possible to devise new solutions to problems. In this way disabled youngsters can participate more in the resources which the community has intended for them.

Following consultations with the local rehabilitation units in the area concerned, the rehabilitation officers have been linked to the experiment as liaison officers.

CONTACTS NEEDED BY A PUPIL

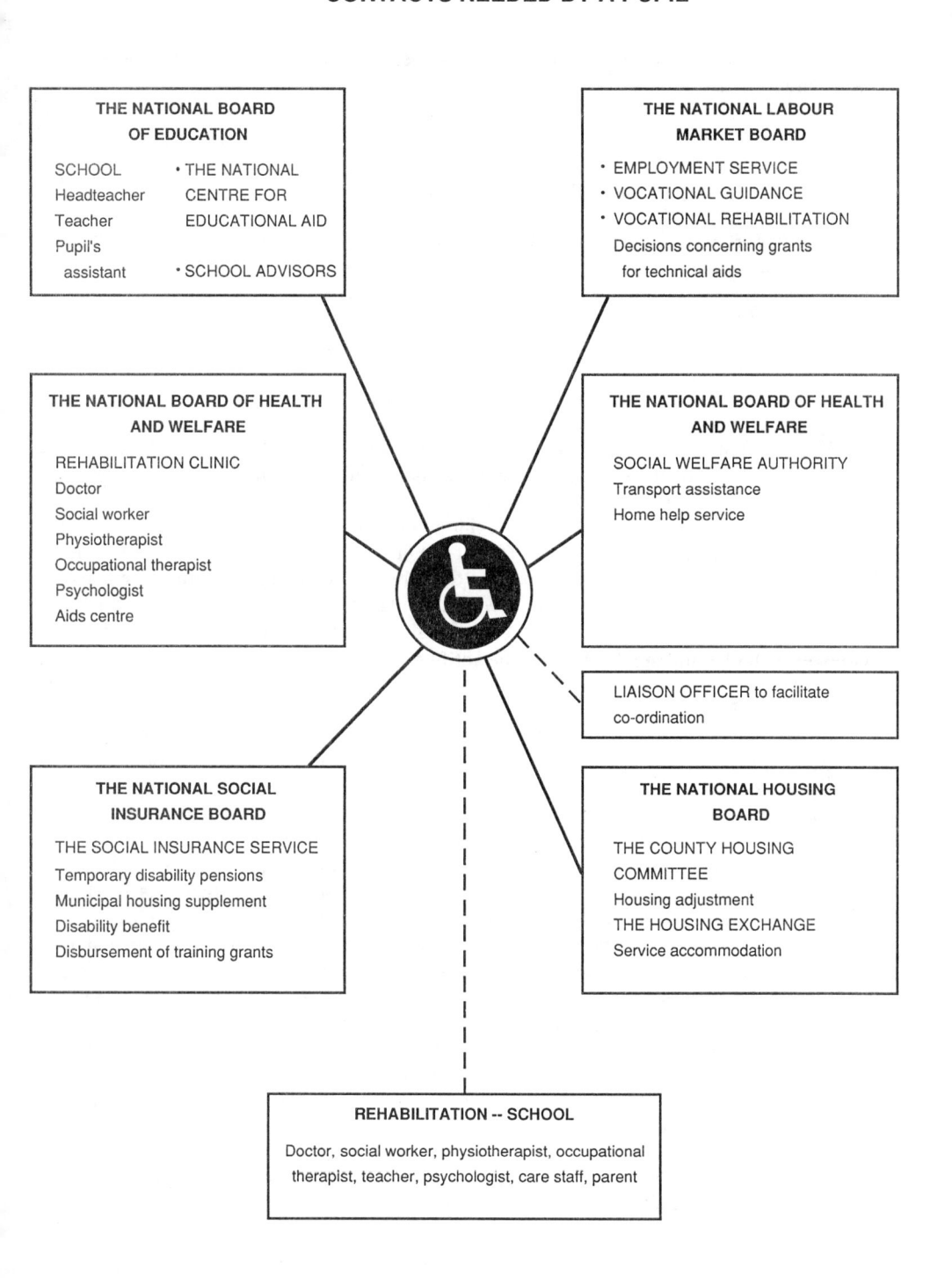

THE NATIONAL BOARD OF EDUCATION

SCHOOL
Headteacher
Teacher
Pupil's assistant

- THE NATIONAL CENTRE FOR EDUCATIONAL AID
- SCHOOL ADVISORS

THE NATIONAL LABOUR MARKET BOARD

- EMPLOYMENT SERVICE
- VOCATIONAL GUIDANCE
- VOCATIONAL REHABILITATION
  Decisions concerning grants for technical aids

THE NATIONAL BOARD OF HEALTH AND WELFARE

REHABILITATION CLINIC
Doctor
Social worker
Physiotherapist
Occupational therapist
Psychologist
Aids centre

THE NATIONAL BOARD OF HEALTH AND WELFARE

SOCIAL WELFARE AUTHORITY
Transport assistance
Home help service

LIAISON OFFICER to facilitate co-ordination

THE NATIONAL SOCIAL INSURANCE BOARD

THE SOCIAL INSURANCE SERVICE
Temporary disability pensions
Municipal housing supplement
Disability benefit
Disbursement of training grants

THE NATIONAL HOUSING BOARD

THE COUNTY HOUSING COMMITTEE
Housing adjustment
THE HOUSING EXCHANGE
Service accommodation

REHABILITATION -- SCHOOL

Doctor, social worker, physiotherapist, occupational therapist, teacher, psychologist, care staff, parent

The Project

The 60 or so young persons taking part were selected in consultation with the rehabilitation advisors and local and regional rehabilitation units.

Following an initial mail shot, the young persons selected were contacted personally and given further information about the project. Appointments were then made for interviews with them and their parents. Since the project would occupy quite a considerable period, it was important for the young persons taking part to be told that they were free to discontinue their contact with the project team when they wished to do so. They could always return later on if they liked. One important part of the project was to help these young persons to feel that they are *personally responsible for the measure needed to be taken.* It was therefore important that they themselves should also decide the amount of dealings they wish to have with us.

Because of this freedom of choice, some young persons who at first were hesitant about taking part, joined the project. Most of the young persons made their decisions after talking the matter over with their families.

The project leader, together with the local liaison officers, visited and interviewed the young persons and their parents in their homes. On these occasions the young persons described their experiences of school and their plans for future education or employment. The interviews followed a set pattern, including questions about school, conditions at home, leisure, preferences concerning future education, employment, etc.

Only a small number of the young persons interviewed stated that they had received any close guidance about planning PRYO. Only a few of the 60 youngsters taking part knew about the information material available at all schools on the subject of planning for employment and the future. They believed that extended PRYO was only available for school-fatigued or disruptive pupils. None of these young persons had been asked whether they needed any technical aid in connection with their intended PRYO period. Those who had personal assistants at school did not know whether their assistants were entitled and able to accompany them to their work experience locations.

Following consultations with the youngsters themselves, the school careers teacher or the SYO officer was contacted in each individual case. All of the persons thus approached were prepared to co-operate. Joint meetings were planned and held. The pupil and, if possible, his parents were always present on these occasions. Schools were represented by the pupil welfare team members who, in the opinion of the careers teacher, had an important part to play in planning. The project team was represented by the liaison officer and the project leader. The school situation of the individual pupil and aspects of future education and employment were discussed on these occasions, and various suggestions and solutions were jointly evolved by the participants.

All of these contacts were then followed up in telephone contacts with both school and pupil. In a number of instances it was also possible for the school advisor to attend, which was an advantage especially during the introductory phase of planning. His knowledge and experience concerning the availability of special solutions came in useful in several cases.

During the year, the liaison officers have kept in continuous touch with both school and pupils, so as to discuss and settle current issues. In some cases the school has suggested follow-up conferences together with the project team, while in other cases the initiative has come from parents or from the liaison officers.

Practically all the parents and young persons we met during our work on the project stated that in their opinion, young persons with orthopedic handicaps encounter more substantial difficulties in the transition between school and employment.

Many of the young persons themselves expressed concern at the risk of not getting a job on completing their education. At a time when job opportunities are in short supply for all young persons, employment prospects for the handicapped are felt to be extremely limited.

The overwhelming majority of the parents felt that the experimental arrangement of a liaison officer had been useful to the youngsters.

In the course of the project, only two young persons chose to discontinue their contacts with the project team, their reason being that they felt themselves to be so slightly handicapped that they did not require any special support for the time being.

Most of the other young persons have spontaneously declared that contact with the project team meant a great deal to them in the process of planning their future education or employment.

Most of the young persons involved in the project have been more or less regularly in touch with rehabilitation units. Some of them have had dealings with other specialists and many have received regular physiotherapy.

Routines for transfer to rehabilitation clinics or long-term care vary somewhat from one hospital management district to another, but in all cases the rehabilitation units lose touch with young persons somewhere between the ages of 18 and 20.

In the course of the project, contact has been maintained with the regional rehabilitation advisors. Co-operation arrangement have varied somewhat between the three experimental areas. In the County of Halland, the rehabilitation advisor has taken part in all visits to schools, and this participation has been of great benefit to the work of the project.

In the other areas, the rehabilitation advisor has arranged special in-service days for school staff who are to receive orthopedically handicapped pupils in their classes. Project personnel and rehabilitation staff have assisted on these occasions.

As the project has progressed, continuous reports have been transmitted between the rehabilitation advisors and the project team.

Co-operation between schools and the project team has run smoothly. Consultations have been held on one or more occasions concerning all the pupils involved in the project.

The arrangements for these consultations have varied, depending on local pupil welfare routines. On certain occasions the entire pupil welfare team has taken part, while on others only the SYO advisor and, where applicable, the class teacher have been involved.

The pupils preferred the latter arrangement. It has been easier for them to assert their views in a smaller group. Even if a pupil gets on well with everybody in the team, it can be rather daunting having to face ten adults on his own. Experience from the project has clearly shown that all planning for these young persons requires a great deal of time. The SYO advisors and careers teacher had to devote a great deal more time to these pupils than to others. The task of finding PRYO/PRAO opportunities requires both a knowledge of the potentialities and limitations of the young persons concerned and time in which to plan PRYO so that it will run smoothly for the individual.

A large number of the young persons taking part broached the idea of extended PRYO when talking to the pupil welfare team, and in most cases this was actually arranged.

As the project proceeded, it became increasingly apparent that the PRYO/PRAO period was of the utmost importance to this category of young persons. Only a small number of them were able to acquire work experience.

All planning for the transition between compulsory and upper secondary schools takes a lot of time and requires extra inputs. A certain amount of handling time was involved in obtaining finance for adjustment measures and approval for the procurement of technical aids. Accordingly, we have tried to begin planning upper secondary studies for young persons involved in this project about one term earlier than we begin making similar plans for other pupils.

In many cases, informal discussions were held between the school and the admissions board and also together with the receiving school, so as to facilitate the transition.

In the case of pupils whose handicaps require extra measures, a "PRYO week" was often arranged at the receiving school so as to give the pupil and the receiving staff an opportunity of talking things over.

Summing up

In the course of the project, we have not come across any organised co-operation between schools and vocational rehabilitation services where handicapped youngsters are concerned. Several of these young persons will in all probability be dependent on vocational rehabilitation resources later on.

According to the description of the project, these activities were expected to make young persons with orthopedic handicaps more prepared for independent living, employment and occupation. The liaison officer, together with the relevant parties, was to take the necessary steps to this end and assist teachers and others in devising means of overcoming problems connected with the integration of orthopedically handicapped pupils.

The reaction we have met from young persons and parents clearly shows that a liaison officer is needed. The experience gained in working together with schools, rehabilitation units and vocational rehabilitation services has shown the model for this work included in the project plan to be viable.

Today, the project is finished. However, in the county councils where the project has been carried on, the work has been made permanent. The permanent organisation is worked out somewhat differently, but the working method and the philosophy are the same as in the project. In the new organisation, the liaison officer has had access to help from occupational therapists and physiotherapists as well.

ACCOMPANYING SERVICES IN FRANCE: REHABILITATION FOLLOW-UP TEAMS

by
Thibault Lambert

Introduction

Co-ordination and management issues were shown to be of particular importance during the OECD/CERI Project on Transition. How were the contributions of different government departments and voluntary agencies made known to young people and their families and put together in a coherent package to facilitate access to training for employment and independent living?

In France, the *Commission technique d'orientation et de reclassement professionnel* (COTOREP) — Technical Commission for Orientation and Professional Rehabilitation — in each *département* (administrative territorial division) offered an interesting model. One of the services available to the Commission is the *Equipe de préparation et de suivi du reclassement* (EPSR) — Team for the Preparation and Follow-up to Rehabilitation. This contribution looks at follow-up services with particular emphasis on the work of EPSR teams.

Transition

The period of transition from school to vocational training and employment is a sensitive one, particularly for young people who are handicapped. The activities of the many agencies need to be more closely co-ordinated by persons or groups who act as guides to accompany individuals and their families through transition. This guidance should not be confined to vocational training and employment but should seek to open up opportunities for social interaction which result in true integration.

The French Context

Two commissions were set up at the département level in 1975 to be responsible for arranging and co-ordinating provision and services for children, young people and adults who are considered to be handicapped.

The *Commission d'éducation spéciale* (CDES) is responsible for planning services, considering the assessed needs of children and young people who require special education and sanctioning or making educational and other arrangements to meet them. The commission is responsible for all such arrangements for individuals up to the age of 20. It delegates its powers to two sub-commissions, one for the pre-school and elementary stages, and the other for the secondary stage.

The second commission is the *Commission technique d'orientation et de reclassement professionnel* (COTOREP). It is responsible for individuals over the age of 20 and develops programmes which include employment, sheltered work, alternatives to work and other facilities and services. The commission also decides who is to be accorded invalidity status and the pensions they are to receive. It thus has a profound influence on the future lives of young people with significant disabilities.

Two considerations need to be borne in mind. First a great deal of provision of all kinds, including education and vocational training is carried out by voluntary associations and agencies which are subsidised by the State social security system. Secondly, there may be a gap, in practice, between the work of the commissions when young people with special educational needs leave the regular school at 16 and do not enter any form of continuing education or training.

Follow-up Services

Within the ambience of the two commissions, three kinds of services carry out a guidance role in different ways. The criteria which distinguish them are:
— Whether they specialise in employment, social integration or both;
— Whether they are linked to an establishment or not. Some facilities for those who are disabled have their own follow-up services. Other agencies have been set up specifically for follow-up work;
— The age range for which they provide a service. Some services help clients of all ages while others concentrate on the needs of adolescents;
— The legal status of the service. Not all services are liable to regulation. Some have an unofficial status being financed from within the general budgets of establishments. Only one service, the EPSR, is subject to specific regulations.

a) **Establishment-linked Follow-up Services**

These have no official status and are limited to three years after children and adolescents leave an institution (Statutory Order 56-284 of March 1956, Annex 24, Article 32). These activities are "subordinated to other initiatives" in the sense that they are not always given priority.

There are different kinds of establishments with such services and it is necessary to distinguish between disabilities; for instance, medico-professional institutes (IMPRO) provide for young people with marked intellectual disabilities up to the age of 20 and in some cases beyond. Some of them have their own follow-up services and this kind of institute is a particularly good example where on average 38 per cent of those who attend are placed and supported in ordinary employment.

Young people with physical and sensory disabilities either attend specialised rehabilitation centres for particular disabilities or general rehabilitation centres. These centres are concerned with direct placement and leave longer-term follow-up and integration to the EPSR.

b) **Independent Guidance and Support Services**

These are created by associations for the disabled to deal specifically with the social integration of individuals.

c) **EPSRs**

These are regulated and are one of a number of services for the adolescent age group. Regulations, orders and circulars in 1975, 1978 and 1979 defined their role, structure and finance. EPSR teams are multi-disciplinary teams to support people who are handicapped and enable them to achieve a stable social and professional life. They participate in every stage of the integration process. They are concerned with transport, housing, psychological preparation and rehabilitation.

EPSR Services

i) **Among the tasks of the teams are**

— To provide individuals with information relevant to rehabilitation;
— To improve vocational and professional competence by arranging for placements in training institutions, sheltered workshops and in work;
— To give vocational guidance and support in employment;
— To work in industry and commerce to inform managers and workers of the potential of handicapped persons and to seek positions for them;
— To establish a dialogue with other professionals about appropriate services and programmes.

ii) **The structure of EPSR services**

There are two kinds of teams, those which have public status and those which have private associative status. Public teams have a minimum of two members, a placement officer and a social worker. They may also have a member for secretarial and information work and a receptionist. Private teams are often made up of four or five persons with similar functions.

Teams have recourse to psychologists, speech and other therapists of all kinds, who can be paid on a sessional basis up to the equivalent of a full-time worker.

EPSRs are set up by the *département* Head for Work and Employment (DDTE) and public teams are fully financed. Private teams receive up to a maximum 75 per cent grant and must raise the rest of their finance from other public and private agencies.

iii) **Statistics**

There are 73 EPSRs of which 50 are public and 23 are private. They cover 70 *départements* with both public and private teams in three of them.

Figures from about twelve teams show that they have more than doubled their number of clients between 1980 and 1985. Two-thirds of them were men and one-third were young people between the ages of 18 and 25. Disabilities were predominantly physical and sensory but about one-third were intellectual disabilities or psychiatric conditions. Approximately 10 per cent of clients had multiple disabilities. Their general education level was limited with only one-third of all applicants having a general education leaving certificate.

Just under half of the applicants underwent rehabilitation and of these 84 per cent obtained open employment, 5 per cent received vocational training and 11 per cent entered sheltered workshops. Other applicants received career guidance, help with housing, transport or leisure activities, family support and other forms of help.

The Activities of the EPSR

It should be recognised that the COTOREP only directs individuals to the team if there is a theoretical likelihood of obtaining employment. The major activities of the teams are preparation, placement and follow-up. Much of the work involves complementing vocational and professional training with work on the social aspects of transition.

i) Preparation

A programme is prepared, with client co-operation and agreement, for each individual. This aims at social and work independence. The planning involves a number of activities such as discussions, exchanges of information and collaboration with local agencies.

Among different aspects of preparation the following are emphasized:

— Psychological preparation which aims to help the individual gain confidence, get rid of psychological blocks and make a dynamic readjustment to his or her disability;
— Social preparation which aims to clarify administrative matters such as pensions and benefit claims and establish status as a person seeking employment. This aspect is to enable individuals to have financial resources, housing, help, where necessary with self-care, and information about rights and needs and thus be in a position to look for a job;
— Preparation for employment which may include short preparation courses (15 days) for those who have never worked and courses in sheltered workshops which are institutions for the vocational training of disabled young people. This also includes making use of measures which facilitate the employment of the young people concerned and helping them to present themselves and write *curriculum vitae*.
— Preparation for independence which includes independent travel, finding one's way about in the community and independence from the family.

ii) Placement

The work of the team includes particular attention to identifying and preparing places in different enterprises. First, there is the need for a knowledge of employment conditions in the area. Then there is an approach to management which will involve explaining disabilities and illustrating potential to work. There will next be information about all the financial and other support arrangements available to employers, including modification of the workplace. Finally the contacts must be personal and those offered for employment must be well prepared.

iii) Follow-up

Two aspects of follow-up are equally important:

— *Employment follow-up.* After placement frequent contacts are maintained with the employer and those in the work situation to deal with difficulties which may arise. This guarantee of a regular follow-up and help with difficulties when they occur is significant in maintaining employment. It may be for a short period of months but also, in some cases, for several years. It may take the form of telephone calls, visits and further work with clients.
— *Social follow-up.* This will involve the team social worker in seeing whether the support network for independent living is appropriate, is working or needs to be modified.

Conclusion

Although EPSR services provide for many young people, there is no systematic follow-up to education and training for many other young people with disabilities. The beginning of some co-ordination between institutions and EPSR follow-up arrangements is evident. A great deal still depends on the interest and good will of the establishment from which a young person leaves, usually a medico-professional institute or rehabilitation centre, in referring individuals to follow-up services and on the ability of those services, particularly EPSR teams, to respond effectively.

DEVELOPING INDIVIDUAL SERVICE PLANS FOR PEOPLE WITH SEVERE DISABILITIES,

MANCHESTER, United Kingdom
TRANSITION FROM SCHOOL TO COLLEGE

by
Mick Molloy

This report is about individual planning services for young people with disabilities. It gives a short presentation of Manchester City followed by some insight into policy in the area of services. The "public's" perspective on the disability issue is then discussed and the general ways in which educationalists can respond to those perspectives. A framework for transition from school to college or adult life and a personal plan that enabled one young man to attend his local college are also presented here.

The City of Manchester

The City has a population of about 460 000. The levels of disadvantage and deprivation are high, with many families living below the poverty line in terms of modern definitions of poverty. In some parts of the City well over 50 per cent of families are below that line.

The national rate of unemployment in 1988 was 11.9 per cent; for the North West region of England it was 14 per cent, and for the City of Manchester 21.1 per cent. In central areas of the City, the statistics indicate that 45 per cent of all males were unemployed. Only a small percentage of youngsters who leave school at 16 enter permanent employment. In 1987, 13 per cent of pupils from mainstream schools went into permanent jobs and 28 per cent continued their education largely in colleges. The rest went on to Youth Training Schemes for 18 months or to the unemployment register. Of the 316 pupils who left special schools, only eight went into permanent employment (2.5 per cent).

All these characteristics have implications for the way the City Council provides and delivers services. The demands for educational services has increased as a result of changes in age structure, unemployment levels and social characteristics at the same time as the resource base has special problems. However, this recognition does not extend to providing sufficient financial resources to tackle them.

Post-16 Educational Services for Disabled People in Manchester

In March 1987 a report on the Development of the Post-16 Provision for Disabled People went to Manchester Education Committee. This report requested:

i) More care supporters (two per year over the next five years);
  ii) Funding for youth workers to ensure that disabled youngsters are integrated into youth clubs;
  iii) Additional funding to enable the twenty or so young people with profound mental handicap who leave special school each year to remain in education after they are 19 and probably until they are 21; and
  iv) A systematic building programme to create more barrier-free environments in our colleges.

These issues are being tackled. If progress is slow it is now clear what is required in this area.

The City Council has a policy on "Recruitment and Selection". This is there to ensure that not only do job descriptions accurately reflect the jobs that have to be done, but that the process of selection is as free of subjective bias as possible. Implied in this process is that more people from minority groups will gain jobs and careers in local government. There is also a policy statement entitled "Equal Opportunity in Employment — A Policy Statement."

Policy statements at the level of intention are of little use if they are not effective. It is therefore important to note that:

  i) A national legal framework which states that learning alongside peers in mainstream schools should be the first choice for disabled pupils;
  ii) A growing number of children, and young people, with significant disabilities are now in mainstream education;
  iii) More parents want to see their disabled children learning alongside their non-disabled peers;
  iv) Children and young people with mental handicap spend some of their time learning alongside their mainstream peers;
  v) 20 per cent of pupils are leaving special schools at compulsory school leaving age (16 years) and going into Post-16 Education in integrated settings;
  vi) Some disabled youngsters attend their local youth clubs;
  vii) Disabled adults attend integrated adult provision;
  viii) Deaf people plea to maintain separate provision for them so their sign language will not disappear; deaf people want to train to be tutors in adult education;
  ix) There is a growing minority of disabled people in paid employment in the Local Education Authority; and
  x) There is a will of elected Counsellors to see more integration take place and emergent policies and strategies that ensure there is a commitment to this happening.

Whilst developments are slow, most disabled pupils and students usually say that they wish to remain in integrated settings once there. If integration is a process, and not a state, then the more we learn how to support disabled pupils and students in open settings, the more our educational services will develop.

What Many of us Take for Granted about Disabled People

An appropriate definition of handicap to start with for the purpose of this report is outlined in an OECD/CERI paper which states:

"One specific aspect of policies bears on the distinction between disability and handicap. This is best illustrated by an example. A young person with a physical or sensory disability may not be able to operate a machine in industry as it is produced for the ordinary employee. However, with today's technology it may be possible to modify its operation so that the disabled individual can use it as effectively as other operators. Failure to make the modifications turns the disability into a handicap. It seems, therefore, important to recognise in all the major fields of education, social welfare and employment, that policies which do not include appropriate situational modifications play their part in increasing the handicapping effects of disabilities and will influence the size of the group described as handicapped."

Generalised definitions of the term "handicap" or "disability" are always inadequate because of the many different situations commonly regarded as "handicapping" or "disabling". Numerous differences exist amongst us all, but these differences are not usually experienced as personal "penalties". It is only when the value attached to the difference by others and society in general is a negative one that this tends to happen. This, sadly, would appear to be a widespread phenomenon and not merely one that is particular to people with visible disabilities.

Educational services have in the past required many disabled young people to leave their usual surroundings and go where the services are provided. That is still widely prevalent. Children and young people go away from home to special residential schools, often in other parts of the country. Many of us, traditionally, have had very low expectations for these pupils and students. Services to them have often relied on the use of "special" buildings on one campus, in which the "special" needs of those young people are supposedly met. Segregation of disabled people whatever their age from non-disabled people carries a number of costs for those segregated:

i) It is sometimes suggested that special "assessment and treatment units" are required. However, the very process of removing a young person from his/her usual setting (the mainstream setting) removes the opportunity to observe and analyse the interaction between the person and his/her environment. Artificial environments should be avoided if at all possible;

ii) Once segregated, opportunities to learn how to adapt to living in the person's local community are drastically reduced;

iii) Segregation makes it difficult to reintroduce a person to less restrictive settings;

iv) Personal relationships, with family, friends, neighbours, are usually disrupted by segregation and can become difficult to re-establish;

v) Segregation often reduces the opportunities to learn appropriate behaviour from non-disabled peers;

vi) There is a danger of segregated settings being used unnecessarily because staff in ordinary settings may become less able or willing to serve people who present a challenge when they know that alternatives exist; and

vii) Segregation, *per se,* contributes to a damaging fall of self-esteem.

Why are disabled people as a group devalued? Why do we seek to reinforce their own doubts? These are not easy questions to answer, but along with the issues to do with the way services are designed, answers are probably to be found in the distorted mental images most of us hold, and the bias in those images against disabled people being valued as competent members of society.

Positive Ways to Respond

One major challenge is to develop service provision that meets people's needs, young or old, in an individual way. The way in which services are provided can inhibit or enhance personal freedom and choice. It is, in the first place, important to ensure that a disabled person has the correct blend of support to sustain a life in the open community. Rarely does one come across a service with aims that recognise the importance to the individual of community participation, but unless a service consciously works to such an aim it is likely that it will quickly develop into a place where disabled people go rather than a service which supports them in their daily living. Once separate service has been established, even if it originally did have clear aims, it can begin to assume a logic of its own.

A powerful way of improving service design is to give the people who deliver services the opportunity to become more aware of the implications of their actions on the people they serve. Specific aims could be to:

  i) Develop staff awareness and understanding of the needs of disabled students;
  ii) Examine some typical institutional constraints; and
  iii) Promote development of student awareness of disability through the tutorial system.

Another way is to give senior staff the opportunity to become directly involved in supporting a disabled person doing routine things in the community.

Planning personal services can benefit people at three different levels within the system:

  i) Disabled people have a better chance of getting what they need if a well-written statement specifies the forms, extent and frequency of various interventions needed;
  ii) Providers know exactly what services they should be providing and in what way they need to be provided; and
  iii) Those paying are able to specify exactly what they expect as outcomes for each service used.

The chances of achieving effective and efficient services are much greater with this approach because there is a mechanism to measure whether or not the expected service is being delivered for a specific amount of money and effort. If personal planning is not viewed as an essential function, providers will continue to operate as they usually do now. A disabled person's needs come to be defined as what a provider has available, not what a person requires to lead a full life.

It is not unusual to find a variety of specific services for disabled people with no arrangements for evaluating their combined effort. Typically the means of "getting on the road" assumes more importance for the planner than where one is going. Whilst the processes and structures of planning are important, these will not necessarily determine the direction planning takes. This is set by the principles used in drawing up plans. It would, for instance, be possible to make a personal plan for someone which excluded more than promoted her/his participation in the community. It is very important to be clear about the principles which are used, and, as the plan unfolds, continue to make sure there is a match between principles, process and outcomes. Everyone should have at least a basic entitlement to:

  i) A presence in the community;
  ii) Opportunities to participate in community life;
  iii) Experiences that make us more competent;
  iv) Situations where we make choices; and
  v) Respect and status.

This is what is needed in working with each disabled person requiring additional support.

Guidelines for Transition from School to Adolescent/Adult Life

In England and Wales the 1981 Education Act and the Special Educational Needs Regulations, 1983, require an annual review of the Statement of Special Educational Needs compiled for individual pupils. Although reflecting the statutory position in England and Wales, the principles are capable of general application. The annual review should be part of the series of a school's planned involvement with parents, seeking to promote confident relationships and full participation by them in the education of their children. The involvement of a young person in the decision-making process is important although there is no statutory provision under the 1981 Education Act for this to happen. The presence of a young person at a review as he/she gets older is desirable. The wishes of the young person should, and those of the parents must, be taken into consideration.

The following procedure creates a framework for leavers' reviews based on legislation and good practice in many special schools in the United Kingdom.

i) **First stage**

There should be a formal process which initiates the pre-leavers' assessment for every pupil for whom a Statement of Special Educational Need is maintained in mainstream or special schools. This should commence in the academic year in which a pupil is fourteen. In England and Wales under the 1981 Education Act a local education authority has a statutory responsibility to carry out a mandatory reassessment during the period of twelve months beginning with the day on which a pupil attains the age of thirteen years and six months.

a) Mandatory reassessment must involve the parents from the outset and use the full procedure laid down in Section 5 of the 1981 Education Act, thus enabling parents to submit written comments or make oral comments which the authority must record. As a prelude to this, it is useful to invite parents, by letter, to the school to discuss the information available to the school with the head teacher. The parents should have the option of involving their child in this discussion. At this meeting:
— The pupil's files should be available for perusal;
— It should be explained that the information has been supplied by professionals from several disciplines;
— The general options apparently open to the pupil should be discussed. A variety of pertinent information brochures, careers leaflets, prospectuses and details of local employment which reflect the options should be given to the parents. Appropriate points of contact (e.g. Careers Officer, Principal of Post-16 establishments) should be given so that parents and the pupil can follow up the options presented; and
— Parents and the pupil should be given the opportunity to make their own suggestions and the head teacher should endeavour to suggest appropriate points of contact for further information where appropriate.

b) Towards the end of the school year there should be an open evening for pupils of this age cohort and their parents. This open evening should have contributions from the Careers Service, providers of a local post-16 provision and the multi-disciplinary team attached to the school and give parents and pupils the opportunity to deepen their knowledge of post-school facilities.

ii) **Second stage**

In the year in which a pupil is fifteen a review should take place, usually not later than the spring term. The purpose of this is to plan with more certainty the future course for the pupil, allowing sufficient time for special provision to be arranged.

a) Whilst the review might include all those included the previous year, in addition to professionals requested to attend by parents, the cost implications need to be borne in mind. Selection by parents and head teacher is important; for instance, it is now that the

health visitor could be involved. She/he can contribute to the assessment and planning for the future by indicating whether or not her/his services, or those of her/his district nursing colleagues, would be appropriate.
b) More specific plans should be drawn up.
c) Should it be considered that there is an eventual need for provision not currently available, this is the time at which such a recommendation should be brought to the notice of the Chief education officer. The likelihood that such a recommendation is to be made, and the reason for it, should be drawn to the attention of local colleges to ensure that every opportunity to secure appropriate local provision has been pursued.

iii) **Third stage**

A review should take place in the autumn or spring term in the year in which a pupil is sixteen. The purpose of this review should be to:
a) Monitor progress;
b) Amend recommendations if necessary;
c) Evaluate work experience placements; these can serve the dual function as a "taster" for the young person and a further platform for assessment; and
d) Finalise plans or suggest further schooling.

Such a framework is important to ensure that the process of planning actually takes place for each pupil.

In July 1986 a new Act of Parliament received the Royal Assent. This is the Disabled Persons Act 1986. Section 3 of that act is intended to help bridge the gap which many disabled young people find on leaving school. It requires local education authorities to notify the Social Services Department of all children aged 14 and over who have Statements of Special Education Needs, at a certain specified time. Those young people concerned must then subsequently be again notified to the Social Services Department nine months before they are expected to leave school so that their needs in relation to other statutory services can be determined. These services in England and Wales are those that are principally available under the Chronically Sick and Disabled Persons Act 1970; these include the provision of recreational activities, television, home helps, travelling assistance, and holidays. Section 5 of the 1986 Act has just come into operation and will affect for the first time all pupils who reach their 16th birthday in the academic year 1990/91. It remains to be seen how effective this act will be; there is a clear intention, however, to develop closer co-operation between the work of the Education Department and the Social Services Department and this must be welcomed.

A Personal Service Plan for Transition from School to College Life

The general backbone of a plan is simple. It follows the outline given in the Education (Special Educational Needs) Regulations 1983 mentioned previously. It is based on reinforcing the ordinary life model and gives:

— A description of the person's unique needs;
— The resources required to meet the needs; and
— An indication of how the resources can be secured.

This particular plan for Paul was produced with Paul and his parents to help him transfer from a segregated residential school setting to an ordinary college of further education. The plan answers four essential questions:

a) What are Paul's needs?
b) What educational provision needs to be made to meet those needs?
c) What additional non-educational provision should be made?
d) Where is the most appropriate place for his educational needs to be met?

The plan is drawn from a real case study. The procedure outlined above was followed, but since Paul was attending a residential school in the south of England (some 300 miles away!), Manchester LEA arranged the meetings. They took place largely in Paul's own home, when he was on vacation, and his local college.

Paul's general needs

Paul is in his final term of compulsory education (16 years). He attends a residential school outside Manchester and has indicated his preference to pursue education until he is 19 years old. He has said that he would like this to be at his local college and, as far as possible, with non-disabled people. He and his parents have decided that for this period at least he should live at home.

Paul is a lively outgoing person whose general abilities and interests are much the same as most young people of his age. He is a person with athatoid cerebral palsy and as a result of this his motor functions are grossly impaired. He uses a wheelchair and requires support when transferring to and from, and to propel it, unless it is electric and even then he has not had experience of moving independently any great distances. It is likely that he will not use public transport. He does travel in a car, provided the support to lift him in and out is there, but he cannot sit unaided and someone has to support him. There is no reason why he cannot use a taxi provided the support is there.

His communication needs

Paul understands everything that is said to him but others have great difficulty understanding what he says due to his impaired articulation. They must be prepared to listen and use contextual cues. He is patient and very tolerant of others. This helps a great deal as does his sense of humour.

His educational needs

a) Paul's attainments in the basic skills of literacy and numeracy, although not low, are at the hesitant stage. He requires practice and support to develop fluency. He has the cognitive ability to write, but his hand movements are severely impaired and he cannot write in the conventional sense. He will therefore require an alternative method of writing. He can type, but the typewriter he uses, an IBM Golfball, hides the print from view. A typewriter with a visual display unit would alleviate this difficulty. Once Paul attends college, tutors should begin to explore with him the potential of the microprocessor as a tool for writing.
b) Paul is also interested in Art, French, Astronomy and Computer studies. He has had little opportunity to experience the resources in his own community and has said that he would like a course to help him achieve this.

The education provision to meet Paul's needs

Paul should, in the first instance, attend a twelve-month bridging course at his local college. His personal plan should aim to:
a) Increase his participation in his local community;
b) Offer him experiences that will make him more independent; and
c) Prepare him for an open college situation.

Within the existing college structure Paul's needs can be met with the following blend of provision:

a) A third of his timetable with the special needs group with opportunities for:
   — Problem-solving learning;
   — Participating in discussion groups on social and life skills training; and
   — Experiencing community facilities.
b) A third of his timetable in open classes related to:
   — Typing;
   — Using microprocessors;
   — Art;
   — Geography; and
   — English and Maths through adult literacy groups.
c) A third of his timetable with his support worker in relation to:
   — Exploration of personal aids;
   — Using the local community; and
   — Independence and personal effectiveness training.

Non-educational provision for Paul

Paul will require the following non-educational provision to meet his needs:
a) *Personal support:* in the first instance a 12-month appointment of a personal supporter for:
   — Open classes;
   — Community settings; and
   — Specialist classes.
This should be provided by his local college. The cost will be reimbursed to the college by the Education Department.
b) *Transport:* Paul will be able to use the college transport for disabled people mornings and evenings. He will also require an allowance to allow him to experience his wider community during the year. This money should be paid to his local college by the Education Department, and will probably be used to purchase taxi time to transport Paul and his supporter into the wider community.
c) *Communication aids:* The provision to meet Paul's needs in this area has been explored by specialists from the district health authority. Paul will initially require equipment from the following sources:
   — Education Department: Brother printer EP22 and a photonic wand both purchased by the Education Department, but remaining the property of Manchester Education Committee when Paul finishes his course. This equipment is for use in college;
   — Department of Health and Social Security: Paul will require similar equipment for personal use at home. This should be pursued through his consultant at Booth Hall Children's Hospital.
d) *Physiotherapy:* Paul should receive termly supervision by the community physiotherapist from the district health authority. This provision should:
   — Assist him with his exercises;
   — Help his parents to support him in his exercises; and
   — Offer training to his personal supporter.
e) *Physical and financial support:* Paul will also require assistance from the Social Services Department in the following areas:

- His home will require modifications to allow him to live with increasing independence. Paul has not lived at home regularly since he was twelve;
- Financial benefits on change of status due to age, especially in relation to Requirement Regulations Schedule 4, paragraph 18 (claims for a permanent helper);
- Independence aids within his home and also in relation to communication aids that cannot be provided by the Department of Health and Social Security; and
- Ensuring that personal support is available to him to pursue his interests after he leaves college.

Reviews of Paul's personal plan

The first review of this plan should take place after the first half-term. It should look at how accurately the picture of Paul's needs is and how well the services respond to them.

Conclusions

The central message of this report is that people with very complicated disabilities can participate in the mainstream of society, if we look closely at the way we deliver the supporting services and ensure that they do support people rather than segregate them. This tends not to happen when "packages" of service provision are based on the institutional model. In the original letter, and not untypically, that was received from the Careers Officer about Paul, many negative stereotypes were used such as: coping with someone (a difficult person); use of term "boy" for a person who is sixteen years old (a child image); removed from his school (segregation); "X" school with all its resources (institutional model of service delivery); and hold out for "Y" college (despair).

What happened to Paul? What about the evaluation? Shortly after Paul had started at college, I moved to another job. The next time I saw him was a year later when he attended a conference as a student delegate on issues to do with disabled students. We spoke briefly and he told me that he was settling into college life. I asked him to keep in touch. About a year later I received a letter done on his own personal computer:

"When I started at Abraham Moss back in 1984 I was on the bridging course, I found the work on the course easy and was not really learning anything and sometimes I got quite bored.

Then in October my tutor got me into some part-time Maths and English classes, in the basic skills area, even though it was only a couple of hours a week I was using my brain more.

In January 1985 I started the 21-hour course doing Maths and English in basic skills. Also I do other studies which are Computers, Social studies and I.E. [Instrumental Enrichment].

Next year I am going onto the CFE [Certificate of Further Education] course which is a one-year examination course and includes the following subjects — Maths, English, Computers, Social Studies and Human Biology, plus French and other subjects to make up the hours."

The point about things being too easy is interesting but Paul was now in an environment where people could respond to that. He had more control over his own studies. Two years after that, I received another letter from Paul. It said:

"I am still at Abraham Moss studying Basic Maths, Basic English and Sociology at GCSE. At the beginning of the academic year I started on the GCSE English but found the level too high. I hope I will be doing GSCE Maths and English next year.

For my sociology I have to do a piece of work in which I have to find information by a number of different sources, such as interviews and questionnaires.

I have decided to do my piece of work about educating the physically handicapped and I wondered if it would be possible for me to interview you on this subject.

I would be very grateful if you could spare the time and it would help me a lot."

That letter speaks for itself. Paul was about to evaluate what I do.

Paul is still pursuing a college course in an open environment. He very firmly wanted to come home and receive his education in his own community. The way forward must be to think positively with individuals about their desirable futures and help them plan them. A starting point might be to suggest that every college should not be allowed to refuse admission to a disabled student other than on the following proven grounds:

— Course is full and there is not an alternative acceptable to the student;
— Prospective student is not qualified for course;
— The degree of personal support required by the student is not available;
— The student does not have the necessary personal aids to have access to the course material;
— The physical barriers on site will make movement in important areas impossible for the student;
— The student could not get to college because no transport is available; and
— That such modifications as might reasonably be made within the college to remove the grounds for refusal have been examined.

Colleges should be rigorous in this approach and should actively assist intending students with counselling or refer them to an appropriate support agency. Analysis of this information will help local authorities with the planning for future resources.

This individual example is a summary of principles put into practice which exemplifies what can be done, even in difficult circumstances, if objectives are clear and actively pursued.

CASE MANAGEMENT IN THE UNITED STATES

by
Ruth Luckasson

The phrase "case management" is used frequently in the United States by individuals in the human service fields. Generally the phrase appears to carry a positive connotation, but its use by many human service workers is often accompanied by an expression of disappointment that case management "does not work as well as it should". Further questioning rarely yields specifics about either the precise definition of case management, why it does not work, or what we could do to improve it. It is as though everything about case management is supposed to be self-evident. But of course it is not.

This report will attempt to analyse some of the case management issues that have arisen in the United States and perhaps provide some useful counterpoints for discussion of the international experience. Regrettably, little empirical or qualitative research has been conducted on case management in the United States. With few exceptions, the writing in the area consists primarily of reports on funded projects, training handbooks, and descriptions of how case management ought to be conducted and what it ought to accomplish. Since much of this literature is unpublished, it is frequently not peer-reviewed, and it is difficult to collect. My own literature search was most fruitful when I was able personally to contact authors who then generously shared their collections with me. For an excellent compilation of literature on the subject, the reader is referred to the bibliography.

The report will begin with a description of the evolution of case management in the United States. Next, it will survey the primary definitions of the phrase and attempt to distill the common themes running through the definitions. It goes on to discuss issues affecting implementation, such as direction, independence, authority, caseload, training, and job satisfaction. Finally, some state-by-state descriptions of case management will be reviewed. Since a convenient access to many of the referenced materials was difficult, excerpts from documents that may suggest useful starting points for discussion were provided.

The Evolution of Case Management

Reviewing the history of the principle of case management in social services suggests that it is not an invention of the 1980s. The idea emerged early in United States' attempts to assist individuals by providing social services. A pioneer of American social work practice, Mary Richmond, emphasized as early as 1922 the importance of what she termed "indirect action" (Richmond, 1922) but what we would probably call case management: "Indirect action through many parts of the social environment — through other persons, through institutions and agencies, through material things — though not the only approach of the social case worker, is more exclusively within his field than are some of the other approaches (i.e. counselling) I have mentioned".

Case management has been rediscovered periodically since then, by different professions, often by different disability groups, and frequently as components of different social policies. For example, the early 1970s saw a modern manifestation of case management principles when Elliot Richardson, then Secretary of Health, Education and Welfare under President Nixon, issued a memorandum entitled "Services Integration: Next Steps". Federally-funded services integration projects, the Services Integration Targets of Opportunity (SITO) Projects, were begun in order to establish inter-agency linkages among human service programmes. The goal was to reduce the dependency of individuals on welfare who had multiple problems by providing: "*a)* the co-ordinated delivery of services for the greatest benefit to the people; *b)* a holistic approach to the individual and family unit; *c)* the provision of a comprehensive range of services locally; and *d)* the rational allocation of resources at the local level so as to be responsive to local needs." (Richardson, 1971, reported in Caragonne and Austin, n.d.). Recently, *The New York Times* discovered case management. An editorial heralded a "bold" alteration to mental health care delivery — a corps of "case managers" to address the needs of people with mental illness. "The experiment deserves local approval and national attention." ("Mental Health on the Street", 1988, p. 22). There must be something about the social problems of individuals and the idea of case management that accounts for its appeal, longevity and adaptability.

Case management appears to have taken root in the modern developmental disabilities field with the birth of de-institutionalisation and the philosophical commitment to providing services consistent with the principles of least intrusion and least restriction. As individuals with developmental disabilities left total-care facilities and began to confront the complexities of a scattered service system, it became clear that most of these individuals would require assistance to create the service package indicated by their needs. At the same time, people with disabilities began to assert their autonomy and decision-making powers, creating a self-advocacy movement. Urging that they be treated as "consumers", self-advocates promoted a shift in the balance of power, recasting human service workers as the employees of the people who have the disabilities, and demanding that decision-making power be in the hands of the disabled person rather than the worker. Given the very real disabilities that self-advocates experience, assistance in the form of a case manager was essential to fulfill the client's intentions and assist him or her in negotiating the complex and often fragmented service system. It has been suggested that increased emphasis on case management generally accompanies theoretical shifts from attempting to change the individual through clinical services to attempting social change of the individual's environment through social manipulation (National Association of Social Workers, 1984).

A related interpretation has been offered. Perhaps after total-care institutions no longer provided the point of accountability for the lives of people with disabilities, it became necessary to designate an alternative point of accountability. A single-service institution could not be held responsible since the needs of people with developmental disabilities require wide-ranging services from many types of service providers. Thus, designating a person, rather than an institution, as the point of accountability satisfied the system's need for pinpointed responsibility. Case managers fulfilled this role.

The phrase "case management" has not been without criticism. The primary objection is that an individual is not a "case" to be "managed". While accepting the sensitive nature of the objection, for ease of communication this report will use the phrase.

What is a Case Manager?

One way to analyse the definition and function of a case manager in the United States is to review the legal mandates for this service and the responses from relevant professional groups. Case management has been described and mandated in many official directives including federal laws, state laws, and court cases, and by professionals in the human services fields. Some examples follow.

The federal Developmentally Disabled Assistance and Bill of Rights Act, major legislation in the disabilities area, was passed in 1975 as an amendment to the Developmental Disabilities Services and Facilities Construction Act. Its purposes were to expand federal assistance to assure that all persons with developmental disabilities receive the services and opportunities necessary to enable them to achieve their maximum potential through increased independence, productivity, and integration into the community; to enhance the role of their families in assisting the person to achieve maximum potential; and to support a system in each state to protect the human and legal rights of persons with developmental disabilities (the state "protection and advocacy" systems, 42 USC 6000 *et seq.*). The statute designates case management as a priority area and defines it as:

> "... activities to establish a potentially life-long, goal-oriented process for co-ordinating the range of assistance needed by persons with developmental disabilities and their families, which is designed to assure accessibility, continuity of supports and services, and accountability and to ensure that the maximum potential of persons with developmental disabilities for independence, productivity, and integration into the community is attained." [42 USC 60001(16°), P.L. 100-146, sec. 102].

Another major disability law, the federal Rehabilitation Act of 1973 (29 USC 701 *et seq.*, P.L. 93-516), was designed to develop and implement, through research, training, services, and the guarantee of equal opportunity, comprehensive and co-ordinated programmes of vocational rehabilitation and independent living. It requires that each consumer be served according to the Individualised Written Rehabilitation Plan. Among the services included by the Act are case management services, "counseling, guidance, referral, and placement services for individuals with handicaps, including follow-up, follow-along, and specific post employment services necessary to assist such individuals to maintain or regain employment, and other services designed to help individuals with handicaps secure needed services from other agencies, where such services are not available under this act." [29 USC 723(a)(2)]

Similarly, the federal Mental Health Systems Act requires that every state provide case management services to chronically mentally ill individuals who receive substantial amounts of public funds or services [42 USC 300x-11(b)(6)(amendment of 1986, P.L. 99-660]. For a fuller discussion of case management services for individuals with mental illness, see Platmman *et al.* (1982).

In the current federal Medicaid health insurance reform proposal, case management services are included as a reimburseable community and family-living service. The Social Security Act defines case management as "services which will assist individuals... in gaining access to needed medical, social, educational, and other services." [42 USC 1396n(g)(2)]

The federal special education statute, the Education for All Handicapped Children Act of 1975 (20 USC 1400 et seq., P.L. 94-142) requires that a handicapped child's education and related services be co-ordinated by an interdisciplinary team according to an Individualised Education Programme (IEP). An IEP is:

"... a written statement for each handicapped child developed in any meeting by a representative of the local educational agency or an intermediate educational unity who shall be qualified to provide, or supervise the provision of, specially designed instruction to meet the unique needs of handicapped children, the teacher, the parents or guardians of such child, and whenever appropriate, such child, which statement shall include *i)* a statement of the present levels of educational performance of such child; *ii)* a statement of annual goals, including short-term instructional objectives; *iii)* a statement of the specific educational services to be provided to such child, and the extent to which such child will be able to participate in regular educational programs; *iv)* the projected date for initiation and anticipated duration of such services; and *v)* appropriate objective criteria and evaluation procedures and schedules for determining, on at least an annual basis, whether instructional objectives are being achieved." [20 USC 1301(19)]

Transition, the process of assisting young people with disabilities to move from special education and school to work, has been the focus of several OECD/CERI studies. Case management forms an essential part of successful transition (a description of current US service systems and concepts in transition can be found in Ludlow, Turnbull, and Luckasson, 1988).

Many states have developed state regulation to accompany federal case management legislation. Minnesota, for example, has attempted to address the issue of case management by mandating that counties provide ongoing case management services to any client diagnosed as mentally retarded or as having a related condition. Case management services are defined as including "diagnosis, an assessment of the individual's services needs, an individual services plan, and methods for providing, evaluating and monitoring the services identified in the plan" [Minnesota Statutes Annotated sec. 256B.092 (1988)]. Minnesota has also legislated an Interagency Office on Transition Services. The office is within the Department of Education and is directed to gather and co-ordinate data on transition services for secondary age handicapped pupils, provide information and technical assistance to state and local agencies involved in transition services from school to work, to assist in establishing local interagency agreements, and to assist in planning interagency training to develop and improve transition services [Minnesota Statutes Annotated sec. 120.183 (1988)].

A federal district court, after ordering the closing of Pennhurst, a large mental retardation institution in southeast Pennsylvania, mandated that the counties appoint case managers to serve the needs of all class members of the Pennhurst case (*Halderman v. Pennhurst,* 1979; Order for the Interim Operation of Pennhurst, March 5, 1979, reported in Conroy and Bradley, 1985). (For a well-researched description of the Pennhurst deinstitutionalisation, see Conroy and Bradley, 1985). The court found that lack of accountability in case management had been the central reason for the lack of movement from institution to the community (Laski and Spitalnik, 1979).

Two major professional groups, the Accreditation Council for Services to People with Developmental Disabilities (ACDD) and the National Association of Social Workers (NASW), have also addressed the principles of case management. A frequently cited definition of case management is found in the standards for accreditation of ACDD. This nationally respected voluntary accreditation group is comprised of the representatives of ten major professional groups in the field of mental retardation. Many service-providing agencies as well as consumers across the country regard the ability to meet ACDD standards as the hallmark of high-quality services. The federal government has, in several notable cases such as Medicaid federal health insurance, adopted ACDD standards as the federal law. ACDD standards emphasize co-ordinated service delivery and the section on plan co-ordination refers specifically to an individual plan co-ordinator or case manager. The relevant standards on case management follow:

"600. An individual program plan co-ordinator is designated for each individual being served. Regardless of who is designated, staff of all agencies providing any component of service required by the plan take an active role in assuring effective communication and overall plan co-ordination.

"605. Each individual unable to function as his/her own individual plan co-ordinator is assigned one who is responsible for monitoring and co-ordinating all activities in implementing the individual plan.

"606. If the individual is not the plan co-ordinator, the individual plan co-ordinator is identified to the individual, to the individual's parents or guardian or advocate, and to those persons who provide services to the individual.

"607. The agency's written procedures allow an individual or an individual's parents, guardian, or advocate to request and secure a different individual plan co-ordinator.

"If the individual is not the plan co-ordinator, the designated co-ordinator:

"608. assists the individual in locating and obtaining, outside or inside the agency, those services identified by the planning team;

"609. observes at least monthly the implementation of programs and the delivery of services, and intervenes to ensure implementation of the individual plan;

"610. facilitates the transfer of the individual to another service or agency when such transfer is desired by the individual and such a transfer is consistent with the individual's plan;

"611. elicits the individual's preferences and respects those preferences when they are not inconsistent with the achievement of goals;

"612. assists the individual in assuming management of those activities for which the individual has demonstrated management capacity." (ACDD, 1988)

The National Association of Social Workers promulgated "NASW Standards and Guidelines for Social Work Case Management for the Functionally Impaired" (November 2, 1984). While recognising that various models of case management are being practiced around the country, and that the case management function is not always carried out by professional social workers, the Association attempted to clarify some of the issues in order to guide social workers in providing case management. Case management was defined as "a mechanism for ensuring a comprehensive program that will meet an individual's need for care by co-ordinating and linking the components of a service delivery system. The components may be in a single agency or may be spread through various agencies. In either instance, sufficient authority must be granted to the case manager to allocate and monitor services if case management is to be effective."

NASW issued three standards to direct the professional behaviour of social workers in the provision of case management services:

"Standard 1. Enhancing self-determination. It is the responsibility of the social worker as case manager to assure that clients are involved, to the greatest possible extent, in the development and implementation of the plans for their care.

"Standard 2. Primacy of the client's interests. The social worker as case manager should use all his or her professional skills to serve a client and should carefully weigh the organization's goals in relation to the client's needs.

"Standard 3. Relationship with colleagues. As case manager, the social worker should treat colleagues with courtesy and respect and strive to enhance interprofessional co-operation on behalf of the client."

NASW further issued five guidelines formulated to direct the process of case management:

"Guideline 1:   Case management tasks. Case management in long term care includes a multidisciplinary assessment of a client and a periodic review of the client's status, the development of a plan of care; implementation of the plan of care, co-ordination and monitoring of services; advocacy, termination of the case, and follow-up.

"Guideline 2:   A shared function. Case management as a function that is shared by the social worker, the client and the client's family, and other professionals and agencies, requires a delineation of tasks.

"Guideline 3:   Accountability and program evaluation. The accountability of the staff and the agency should be assured through appropriate documentation and data collection and through periodic evaluation of the quality, adequacy, and effectiveness of the case management system and of the services provided through this system.

"Guideline 4:   Development of resources and social action. Because a wide range of social and health care systems must be available to assist the functionally impaired and their families, the social worker as case manager must be able to identify gaps in services and work toward the expansion or establishment of services in the agency and in the larger community to meet these needs.

"Guideline 5:   Agency policies and resources. The many unique responsibilities of case management must be backed up by administrative and fiscal support and must be given appropriate consideration in the agency's planning, policy making, staffing, and budgeting processes." (NASW, 1984)

How is a case manager different from a traditional social services worker? Caragonne and Austin suggest this comparison:

Traditional	**Case management services**
8:00 - 5:00.	Indeterminant.
Routine schedule.	Non-routine work.
Operates in office.	Community-based.
One service emphasis.	Multi-service emphasis.
Little or no inter-agency contact	Extensive and varied inter-agency contact
Authority on case-load only.	Authority to represent agency.
Limited decision-making.	Extensive decision-making.
Limited freedom to operate.	Extensive freedom to operate.
Routine feedback.	Periodic, extensive feedback.

Common Themes in Case Management Formulations

Upon reflection, several common themes emerge from the various formulations of case management described in the previous section. All of the formulations anticipate an individualised assessment and evaluation process designed to determine the needs of the individual. It also seems clear that the general purpose of case management is to improve the functioning of the individual, increase his independence and opportunities for a self-directed life, and to provide continuity of care. Undergirding these goals for the individual appears a strong push to distribute social services, both specialised and generic, in a manner as efficient, fair, and rational as possible. All agree that many individuals with developmental disabilities will require a complex array of services over a long period of time, thus resources and services must be genuinely available or there will be nothing to "manage". Finally, there appears to be general agreement that following up on the services received and monitoring the quality of those services are essential components of case management.

Ross (National Conference on Social Welfare, 1981, p. 106) suggested three models for case management programmes, the minimal model, the co-ordination model, and the comprehensive model. He proposed the following comparison:

Minimal model	Co-ordination model	Comprehensive model
Outreach.	Outreach.	Outreach.
Client assessment.	Client assessment.	Client assessment.
Case planning.	Case planning.	Case planning.
Referral to service providers.	Referral to service providers.	Referral to service providers.
	Advocacy for client.	Advocacy for client.
	Direct casework.	Direct casework.
	Developing natural support systems.	Developing natural support systems.
	Reassessment.	Reassessment.
		Advocacy for resource development.
		Monitoring quality.
		Public education.
		Crisis intervention.

Controversies in Case Management

Review of the available literature suggests that several areas arise repeatedly as areas of tension in case management. These include: conflicts between the individual's judgement and the case manager's judgement; whether case managers ought to be independent or part of a service agency; whether case managers can effectively function solely on their personal negotiating skills or whether they must have genuine authority; whether case management responsibility ought to be designated in an individual or a team; what the optimum case management case-load is; and job satisfaction for case managers.

The possibility of conflicts between the individual's judgement and the case manager's judgement has been recognised by most authors. Resolution of conflicts specifically within the case management arena has not been the subject of published research.

Should case managers be independent or part of a direct service agency? The most frequently recognised drawback to case managers being part of a service-providing agency is the potential for conflict of interest (Bersani, 1988; Spitalnik, 1981). This conflict may arise in at least three ways: the manager's loyalty may be divided between his employer and his client; the manager's loyalty may be divided between two clients of the agency; and the manager may limit his selection of services to the services provided by the agency by whom he is employed.

Forcing case managers to be separate from direct service agencies may, however, cause other problems. Such separation may make their professional positions unnecessarily precarious, unnecessarily isolated from the services they are supposed to be managing, and may deny them the "clout" necessary to negotiate their duties. When case management is a separated service, "privatisation" may occur, and non-governmental providers may sell the service under contract to the government. Spitalnik (1981) suggests that private providers of case management services are less desirable than government providers because they lack the institutional stability, permanency, and continuity provided by government services. Another important consideration is that under the US Constitution, important civil rights protections may be limited to the "State action" created by a government provider. Without those civil rights protections, individuals with disabilities are vulnerable to discrimination.

Clearly, case managers must have the ability or clout actually to accomplish the tasks required by their role. This means that in addition to granting them the necessary power, they must be accorded sufficient professional status. One means for assuring that case managers have the power to accomplish their goals is to develop formal inter-agency agreements concerning the receiving agency's acceptance of clients into their programmes. Some creativity may be lost, but the case manager may be spared some of the case-by-case negotiation or "re-litigation" otherwise required in every new situation.

Most authors in the developmental disabilities field suggest that case management responsibilities should be vested in an individual rather than a team. However, Test (1979) reports that in the mental illness field, team structure provides more consistent availability and continuity not dependent on a single case manager, better planning because of the additional points of view, and less "burn-out".

Questions of optimum case management case-loads rise frequently. The report from the State-of-the-art conference indicates that "no other issue was raised with equal consistency or discussed with equal vehemence" (National Conference, 1981, p. 10). Reports from across the states demonstrate that there is enormous variability, with the highest over 100 clients per manager. Later descriptions of case-loads as high as 300 are reported in Spitalnik and Sullivan (1988, p. 27). The judge in the Pennhurst case mandated a case-load of no more than 40. The feedback from the Pennhurst case managers was that a more realistic load would have been 25. Case-load size depends, of course, on the nature of services being provided, the needs and demands of the clients, geographic considerations, and the skill and experience of the case manager. Weighting systems might usefully take into account such factors in the allocation of loads among managers.

The costs of case-loads that are too high include being constantly "on the run" and unable to develop relationships with the clients, always reacting to emergencies rather than helping clients plan for anticipated problems, and responding to the most insistent clients rather than fairly to all the clients. On the other hand, case-loads that are too low will drive up costs and perhaps generate dependence in clients who are too indulged by their case managers.

The job satisfaction of case managers was researched by Caragonne and Austin (n.d.). They report that case managers who expressed high job satisfaction reported high values on mediation skills, persuasiveness, flexibility, and knowledge of inter-agency policies. Satisfaction was positively correlated to greater numbers of inter-agency contacts, ability to receive referrals and to make referrals, and high levels of task feedback, task independence, and self-actualisation (p. 129).

Current Practice

Several representative US case management systems will briefly be described, including California, North Carolina, Colorado, Florida, Eastern Nebraska Community Office of Retardation (ENCOR), and South Carolina. (The information was collected in 1980. For more detail, the reader should consult National Conference on Social Welfare, 1981, pp. 2.2-2.19). A recent three-year study of case management in New Jersey will then be reviewed.

California has 21 "regional centers" employing approximately 1 000 case managers, each manager serving about 64 clients. The regional centres are private non-governmental agencies which contract with the state to provide the services. The regional centre system began as a pilot study in 1966. Two special programmes train parents of persons with disabilities to be case managers. Great variation exists among the 21 centres.

North Carolina does not have a state-wide case management system, but it has five programmes serving eleven counties. The Craven County DD Case Management System has five staff members, each of whom serves approximately 105 individuals. An identified weakness is that since case management in North Carolina has no basis in state law, there is a perceived lack of legitimacy.

Colorado has had a state-wide case management system since 1978, operated through 22 private not-for-profit boards under contract to the state. There are approximately 130 case managers, each serving approximately 65 clients. The boards also provide direct services and consequently, conflicts of interest have been identified.

Florida state law has mandated case management services since about 1977. There are approximately 165 case managers, with case-loads of 105 each. The system is operated out of the State Department of Health and Rehabilitative Services. Identified as the greatest strength of the Florida system is the authority and clarity accompanying the fact that all financial control is within the state agency.

In *Nebraska,* case management has been a component of the widely respected ENCOR since its inception in 1971. The five-county programme employs about 25 case managers, each serving approximately 37 clients. Administratively, there appears to be greater accountability to the counties than to the state.

South Carolina has operated a state-wide case management system out of the Governor's Office since 1980. There are 13 case managers, each with a case-load of approximately 35. The rural nature of the state creates problems in the delivery of services. The placement of the system within the Governor's Office is regarded as politically neutral. Case managers are given great discretion in the purchase of services, and this is regarded as enhancing staff morale and avoiding staff burnout.

New Jersey: one of the best analyses of a US case management system can be found in a recent report on the New Jersey experience (Spitalnik and Sullivan, 1988). New Jersey completed a three-year study of their case management system. Dr. Deborah Spitalnik, Director of the University Affiliated Program (UAP), Robert Wood Johnson Medical School, University of New Jersey, conducted the study. Currently, New Jersey has approximately 25 000 individuals receiving case management services. The study was prompted by the state's rapid de-institutionalisation, making case management increasingly critical for individuals with mental retardation entering the community for the first time; and New Jersey's expansion of eligibility for case management from a typically restrictive definition of mental retardation to the more expansive definition of developmental disabilities.

New Jersey analysed its current case management practice by a variety of methods, including:
"— Interview of case management staff at all levels within the Division of Developmental Disabilities (DDD);
— Interviews of Special Child Health Services case managers;
— Interviews of service providers within the state;
— A detailed survey of area supervisors within DDD;
— A three-tiered consumer survey of direct consumers, family members, and skill-development home providers;

— A review of an unpublished DDD 1985 internal audit of community services case management and intake units;
— A review of the DDD five-year plan;
— A review of the Public Advocate's 1984 survey of community residential facilities for the mentally retarded;
— A review of a monitoring study of mentally retarded clients placed in the community;
— Consideration of the recommendations of the governor's taskforce on services for persons with disabilities;
— A detailed training needs analysis based upon feedback from participants in UAP training programs;
— A survey of case managers' perceptions of the Individual Habilitation Plan currently in use;
— Analysis of the requests to the UAP for technical assistance;
— Collaborative efforts with DDD staff and other service providers." (Spitalnik and Sullivan, 1988, p. 4)

Based on the extensive study, Spitalnik and Sullivan concluded that while the system was functioning adequately from the perspective of most current consumers, there was serious overload from the perspective of the staff. Dysfunction in the service delivery area was summarised:

"— Discontinuity between service need information and system planning;
— Overlapping service provision;
— Restrictive practice in service provision;
— Lack of specialised assessment and program resources;
— Lack of access to generic resources;
— Poor implementation of inter-agency agreements."

Factors which impact negatively on case managers' ability to function effectively include:

"— Lack of clarity of role expectations to workers and to the public;
— Lack of empowerment of case managers;
— High case-loads;
— Paperwork requirements;
— Need for enhanced supervisory structure;
— Need for ongoing in-service education;
— Need for enhanced support services."

The study goes on to make approximately 35 specific recommendations for improving the system. Clearly, the New Jersey Developmental Disabilities Council is pursuing improvement in the provision of case management services to individuals with developmental disabilities.

Conclusion

Ultimately, the real question is how to provide the best case management services in a manner most conducive to successful community integration for individuals with disabilities. The research of Caragonne and Austin suggests that the following characteristics of the work environment lead to increased case management:

"— Tasks are clearly defined by upper level management;
— Leadership providing structure and support;
— High levels of autonomy;

- Little control of behavior through rules and regulations;
- Clear communication patterns between organizational levels;
- Tasks of case management supported within the work environment;
- Commitment to and involvement with the job of case management;
- Sanction to perform tasks in an unorthodox, innovative manner." (p. 115)

Successful community integration for people with developmental disabilities will depend on good case management services. All of our other work to assist in creating genuine opportunities for rich lives in the community will fail if we neglect this task. The issue warrants our best efforts.

BIBLIOGRAPHY

Abrahams, L. and Seidl, H. (Eds.) (1979). *Introduction to Effective Case Management: Guidelines for Effective Communication,* Brown County Community Mental Health, Developmental Disabilities, and Alcohol and Drug Services Board, Wisconsin.

ACDD Accreditation Council on Services for People with Developmental Disabilities (1988). *1990 Standards for Services for People with Developmental Disabilities,* the Council, Boston.

Altshuler, S. and Forward, J. (1978). "The inverted hierarchy: A case manager approach to mental health services", *Administration in Mental Health,* 6(1), 57-58.

Austin, D. and Caragonne, P. (1980). "Analysis of the function of the case manager in four mental health social services setting", *Case Management Project,* University of Texas, Austin, TX.

Austin, D. and Caragonne, P. (1980). "Comparative analysis of twenty-two setting using case management components", *Case Management Project,* University of Texas, Austin, TX.

Baker, J., Intagliata, J. and Kirshtein, R. (1980). "Case management evaluation: Phase one final report" (Executive summary), TEFCO Services, Inc., New York State Office of Mental Health, Buffalo, NY.

Bersani, H. (1988). "Issues in quality assurance in residential services", *TASH, The Association for Persons with Severe Handicaps Newsletter,* 14(10), 2.

Bradley, V. and Conroy, J. (1986). *Community Options: The New Hampshire Choice,* Developmental Disabilities Council, Concord, NH.

Bruininks, R., Meyers, C.E., Sigford, B. and Lakin, K.C. (1981). *Deinstitutionalization and Community Adjustment of Mentally Retarded People,* American Association on Mental Deficiency, Washington, D.C.

Bruininks, R.H., Thurlow, M.A., Thurman, S.K. and Fiorelli, J. (1980). "Deinstitutionalization and community services", in Wortis, J. (Ed.), *Mental Retardation and Developmental Disabilities — An Annual Review,* XI., Brunner/Masel, New York.

"California Association for the Retarded" (memorandum), in: Lueger, S.A. (1981). *Case Management for the Developmentally Disabled: A Background Paper,* Department of Social and Rehabilitation Services, Topeka, KS.

Caragonne, P. and Austin, D. (n.d.). *Final Report: A Comparative Study of the Functions of the Case Manager in Multipurpose, Comprehensive and in Categorical Programs,* School of Social Work, University of Texas, Austin, TX.

Caragonne, P. (1980). "Implementation structures in community support programs: Manpower implications of case management systems". Manpower Development Project, Mental Health Program Office, Tallahassee, FL.

Case Management Committee (1980). *Case Management Services for Developmentally Disabled Persons in Colorado: A Model and Implementing Manual,* Division for Developmental Disabilities, State of Colorado, Denver, CO.

Center for Urban Affairs and Community Services (1978). *Case Management for the Developmentally Disabled: A Feasibility Study Report,* Raleigh, NC.

Clarence N., York Associates (1985). *A Study to Monitor the Status of Mentally Retarded Clients Placed in the Community as Mandated by Public Law 1983, Chapter S24,* Division of Mental Retardation, New Jersey Department of Human Services, Trenton, NJ.

Conroy, J. and Bradley, V. (1985). *The Pennhurst Longitudinal Study: A Report of Five Years of Research and Analysis.* Temple University Developmental Disabilities Center, Philadelphia, Human Services Research Institute, Boston.

Cooney, L. and Smith, C. (1979). *Illinois Case Management Study,* Illinois Governor's Planning Council on Developmental Disabilities, Springfield, IL.

Developmentally Disabled Assistance and Bill of Rights Act, 42 USC 6000 et seq., P.L. 100-146.

Dormady, J. and Gatens, M. (1980). *Case Management: Issues and Models.* State of New York Board of Social Welfare, New York.

Education for All Handicapped Children Act, 20 USC 1400 et seq., P.L. 94-142.

Florida Department of Health and Rehabilitative Services (1983). *Improving Casework and Client Care,* Brehan Institute for Human Services, Tallahassee, FL.

Flynn, R.J. and Nitsch, K.E. (1980). *Normalization, Social Integration, and Community Services,* University Park Press, Baltimore.

Ganser, L.J. (1977). *Case Management Materials,* Division of Community Services, State of Wisconsin Department of Health and Social Services, Madison, WI.

Governor's Task Force on Services for Disabled Persons (1987). *Certain Unalienable Rights* (Final Committee Report) Trenton, NJ.

Graham, J.K. (1980). "The work activities and work attitudes of case management staff in New York State community support systems". New York State Office of Mental Health: Bureau of Program Evaluation, Albany, NY.

Halderman v. Pennhurst State School and Hospital, 612 F. 2d 84 (3rd. Cir. Ct. App. 1979).

Hennessy, S. (1978). "A study of the attitudes of public social workers towards case management" (Doctoral dissertation), University Microfilms International, Ann Arbor, MI.

Hightower-Vandamm, M. (1981). "Case management — A new dimension to an old process", *The American Journal of Occupational Therapy,* 35(5), 295-297.

Horejsi, C.R. (1975). "Deinstitutionalization and the development of community based services for the mentally retarded: An overview of concepts and issues", University of Montana, Missoula, Mont., Project on Community Resources and Deinstitutionalization (Grant N° 90-C-341), Office of Child Development, US Department of Health, Education, and Welfare.

Intagliata, J. (1981). "Operationalizing a case management system: A multilevel approach". *Case management: State of the Art,* National Conference on Social Welfare, Springfied, VA; National Technical Information Service, US Department of Commerce.

Intagliata, J. (1982). "Improving the quality of community care for the chronically mentally disabled: The role of case management", *Schizophrenia Bulletin,* 8(4), 655-674.

Intagliata, J. and Baker, F. (1983). "Factors affecting the delivery of case management services for the chronically mentally ill", *Administration in Mental Health,* 11(2), 75-91.

Jaslow, R.I. and Spagna, M.B. (1977). "Gaps in a comprehensive system of services for the mentally retarded", *Mental Retardation,* 15(2), 6-9.

Johnson, P.J. and Rubin, A. (1983). "Case management in mental healh: A social work domain?", *Social Work,* 26(1), 16-24.

Johnson, T. (1984). *An Evaluation of the Case Management System for People with Developmental Disabilities in Dane County,* Wisconsin Coalition for Advocacy, Madison, WI.

Kahn, L. (1978). *A Case Management System for the Mentally Retarded Citizens of Rhode Island: A Model, a Needs Assessment and Recommendations,* Rhode Island Department of Mental Health, Retardation, and Hospitals.

Koff, T.H. (1981). "Case management in long term care: Assessment, service coordination", *Hospital Progress,* 62(10), 54-57.

Kraber, J.M. (1982). "Case management as a therapeutic tool", *Hospital and Community Psychiatry,* 33(8), 665.

Lamb, H.R. (1980). "Therapist-case managers: More than brokers of services", *Hospital and Community Psychiatry,* 31(11), 762-764.

Landis, S. and Kahn, L. (1978). *Case Management Service: Request for Proposal Guidelines,* Division of Mental Retardation/Development Disabilities, Ohio Department of Mental Health/Mental Retardation.

Laski, F. and Spitalnik, D. (1979). "A review of Pennhurst implementation", *Community Services Forum,* 1(1), 1, 6, 8.

Levine, I. and Fleming, M. (1984). *Human Resource Development: Issues in Case Management,* Center of Rehabilitation and Manpower Services, University of Maryland, College Park, MD.

Levine, M. (1979). "Case management: Lessons from earlier efforts", *Evaluation and Program Planning,* 2, 235-243.

Lippman, L. (1975). *Long Term Personal Program Coordination,* Developmental Disabilities Council of New Jersey, Trenton, NJ.

Louisiana Office of Mental Retardation and Developmental Disabilities (1985). *Case Management Manual,* the Office, Baton Rouge, LA.

Ludlow, B., Turnbull, A. and Luckasson, R. (Eds.) (1988). *Transitions to Adult Life for People with Mental Retardation: Principles and Practices,* Paul H. Brookes, Baltimore, MD.

Lueger, S.A. (1981). *Case Management for the Developmentally Disabled: A Background Paper,* Mental Health and Retardation Services, Department of Social and Rehabilitation Services, Topeka, KS.

MacEachron, A., Pensky, D. and Hawes, B. (1986). "Case management for families of developmentally disabled clients: An empirical policy analysis of a statewide system", in J. Gallagher and P. Vietze (Eds.), *Families of Handicapped Persons: Research, Programs and Policy Issues,* Brookes, Baltimore.

Mather, S., Breedlore, L., Johnson, T. and Wittner, C. (1982). *A Review of Dane County's Case Management System for People Who Are Developmentally Disabled,* Association for Retarded Citizens, Wisconsin.

"Mental health on the street", *The New York Times,* (Jan. 25, 1988), p. 22.

Mental Health Systems Act, 42 USC 300x *et seq.* (amendment of 1986), P.L. 99-660.

Middleton, J.E. (1985). *Case Management in Mental Retardation Service Delivery Systems: a View from the Field.* (Doctoral dissertation), University of Pennsylvania, PA..

Minnesota Statutes Annotated sec. 120.183 (West Cum. Supp. 1988).

Minnesota Statutes Annotated sec. 256B.092 (West Cum. Supp. 1988).

Missouri Department of Mental Health, Division of Mental Retardation/Developmental Disabilities (1984). *Case Management Process Requirements: User's Guide,* the Department, St. Louis, MO.

NASW National Association of Social Workers (1984). *NASW Standards and Guidelines for Social Work Case Management for the Functionally Impaired,* the Association, Silver Spring, MD.

National Conference on Social Welfare (1981). *Final Report: Case management: State of the Art,* the Conference, Washington, D.C.

New Jersey Department of Human Services (1983). "Phase two: Restructuring for service, a plan to improve New Jersey's mental retardation system. Fiscal year 1984-fiscal year 1989", Division of Mental Retardation, Department of Human Services, Trenton, NJ.

Novak, A.R. and Heal, L.W. (1980). *Integration of Developmentally Disabled Individuals into the Community,* Brookes, Baltimore.

Office of Training and Staff Resources (1985). *Case Management Training Curriculum,* Texas Department of Mental Health and Mental Retardation, Austin, TX.

Platman, S., Dorgan, R., Gerhard, R., Mallam, K. and Spiliadis, S. (1982). "Case Management of the Mentally Disabled", *Journal of Public Health Policy,* 3(3), 302-314.

Public Law 98-527, October 19, 1984. *Developmental Disabilities Act of 1984.* US Government Printing Office, Washington, D.C.

Regional Institute of Social Welfare (1977). *The Case Management Model: Concept and Process Definition. Vol. I: Concept and Process Definition; Vol. II: Implementation Requirements; Vol. III: Trainer's Guide,* Athens, GA.

Rehabilitation Act of 1973, 29 US 701 et seq., P.L. 93-516.

Rehab Group Inc. (1984). *Specifications for a System of Individual Service Coordination for Persons With Developmental Disabilities,* Falls Church, VA.

Report to the Congress by the Comptroller General of the United States. *Summary of a Report —Returning the Mentally Disabled to the Community: Government Needs to do More,* HRD-76-152A.

Richmond, M. (1922). *What is Social Case Work? An Introductory Description,* Russell Sage Foundation, New York.

Riffer, N. and Freedman, J. (1980). *Case Management in Community Based Services: A Training Manual,* New York State Office of Mental Health, Albany, NY.

Ross, H. (1980). *Proceeding of the Conference on the Evaluation of Case Management Programs* (March 5-6, 1979), Volunteers for Services to Older Persons, Los Angeles, CA.

Savage, V.T., Novak, A.R. and Heal, L.W. (1980). "Generic services for developmentally disabled citizens". *Integration of Developmentally Disabled Individuals Into the Community,* Novak, A. Riaud Heal, L.W. (Eds), Brookes, Baltimore.

Schwartz, S., Goldman, H. and Churgin, S. (1981). "Case Management for the chronic mentally ill: Models and dimensions", *Hospital and Community Psychiatry,* 33(12), 1006-1009.

Sigelman, C., Bell, N., Schoenrock C., Elias, S. and Danker-Brown, P. (1978). *Alternative Community Placements and Outcome.* Paper presented at the Annual Meeting of the American Association on Mental Deficiency, Denver, Colorado.

Spitalnik, D. (1981). "The case manager role and the training of case managers", *National Conference on Social Welfare — Final Report: Case Management: State of the Art 47-71,* the Conference, Washington, D.C.

Spitalnik, D. and Sullivan, D. (August 1988). *Draft report: Case Management Services for Persons with Developmental Disabilities in New Jersey: A Systems Analysis,* University Affiliated Program, Robert Wood Johnson Medical School, Piscataway, NJ.

Stein, L. (Ed.) (1979). *Community Support Systems for the Long-Term Patient,* Jossey-Bass, San Francisco.

Test, M. (1979). "Continuity of care in community treatment" in Stein, L. (Ed.), *Community Support Systems for the Long Term Patient,* Jossey-Bass, San Francisco.

Turner, J. (1977). "Comprehensive community support systems for severely disabled adults", *Psychosocial Rehabilitation Journal,* 1, 39-47.

United States Senate, Committee on Labor and Human Resources (1979). *Rehabilitation, Comprehensive Services and Developmental Disabilities Legislation: A Compilation,* US Government Printing Office, Washington, D.C.

Willer, B. and Intagliata, J. (1984). *Promises and Realities for Mentally Retarded Citizens,* University Park Press, Baltimore, MD.

Wray, L. and Wieck, C. (1985). "Moving persons with developmental disabilities toward less restrictive environments through case management", in Lakin, C. and Bruinick, R. (Eds.). Strategies for *Achieving Community Integration of Developmentally Disabled Citizens,* Brookes, Baltimore, MD.

Part III

CONCLUSIONS

ESSENTIAL ELEMENTS IN MANAGING TRANSITION

The key message of this report is that young people with disabilities need a continuity of support if they are to make a successful transition to adult life. It is crucial that departments, agencies and professionals work to agreed ends to provide this continuity so that independence in working life can be achieved by all.

Introduction

The closing of this phase of the project on the transition to working life of disabled people, as agreed at the outset, was a meeting of experts, in Denmark. Their role was to identify the most significant issues that are seen to be necessary to ensure the optimal management of this key period in the lives of disabled people.

At the meeting, following an extensive discussion of the case studies that have been reported in Part II, differences in opinion were expressed but consensus emerged over the conditions that are necessary to achieve a smooth transition from school to work for disabled people. The case studies themselves describe a variety of approaches to managing transition in certain Member countries and they illustrate how varying methods have developed in different contexts.

It emerged that the *Kurator* system as developed in Denmark was an important basis from which to evaluate different approaches and to identify significant case management issues. It was agreed that the *Kurator* system came closest to the most ideal arrangement and inevitably this model was clearly highly influential on the more general recommendations that follow.

The conclusions reached at this meeting are intended to be generalisable and are therefore stated rather broadly.

Main Conclusions

Areas of general agreement

It is important to stress that goals for individual disabled people can only be realised within the appropriate social framework and policies of a country, such as those that exist in certain Scandinavian countries. Some of the manifestations of such policies are goals which emphasize fairness, access to the benefits of society that are generally available to all, as well as inclusion and participation in the development of the policies themselves. The realisation of these policies implies the right to full adult status with the pleasures and the pain, the privileges and responsibilities that that concept entails. A society must allow for the full development of all of its citizens and these rights should be reflected in its policies. It has to be recognised, however, that full participation is an action which must also be strived for by individuals and their families. Segregated provision, of any sort, is therefore in opposition to these goals.

In order to achieve these goals it was agreed that the general approach to young people who are disabled should:
— Be individualised, flexible and interactive;
— Give adequate attention to psycho-social factors;
— Involve a planned progression, continuity, follow-up and accountability;
— Involve young people and their families in decision-making.

Furthermore, it has to be recognised and stressed that services will need to continue to be available and that these must have their focus in the neighbourhood and the community.

The organisation of services

The identification of services as an important aspect of successful transition clearly raises the question of how these services should be organised. It was agreed that:

a) They should be planned and provided in such a way that the individual transitional arrangements are not only possible but an integral part of the service delivery system. This means that they must be client-led to allow for a maximum degree of choice for the client. This itself requires a co-ordination of funding arrangements between services and agencies in addition to co-ordinated funding for individuals for the effective management of transition. Furthermore, the system must be flexible enough to be able to respond to the changing pattern of needs of the local community. This in turn means that resources and decision-making should ideally be delegated to the local level.

b) These services should be operated by key-workers who themselves have particular needs:
   i) They require appropriate training;
   ii) They need small case loads since it is essential that support be given, not only to the client, but also to his family and, under these circumstances, cases can become especially complex;
   iii) They need easy access to wide-ranging information on, say, all available programmes and resources;
   iv) They need a professional support group, not only to maintain up-to-date knowledge and to develop skills, but also to increase job satisfaction and to help to prevent "burn-out". There was some discussion over the preferred title to be used for this type of person. It was agreed that the name was important but the actual choice would clearly need to reflect the cirumstances in each Member country.

c) The arrangements must be closely monitored and evaluated to ensure, for example, continuity for clients across different case managers and in the programmes and services available as well as in the handing over, where necessary, from one agency to another. It would of course be preferable for cases to be handled by a single individual.

d) A decision must be made over the range and scope of the case management function during transition. One arrangement may limit the process to one which ensured access to the appropriate facilities, while a different plan might well include an advisory and counselling role. The age range of the client group would also need to be agreed.

A further very important question indeed is whether or not the case management practice should only be related to the employment objective. For instance, should the case manager also be concerned with the adjustment issues involved when a disabled adult moves from the institution to the community. The experience of the *Kurator* model has shown that there is pressure to extend the role of this manager to a wide range of disabling conditions such as severe mental retardation, thus going well beyond the initial brief of working with young people with moderate learning difficulties.

The quality of the manager

There is also a need to look at the qualities of the managers themselves. The following is an outline of some of the major features that such individuals would ideally possess, how they would operate and what they would do.

QUALITIES	Experience with young people in school and elsewhere on a regular basis.
	Social flexibility.
	Good communicator in many different fields of home, school, and work.
	Lives in and knows the area.
	A good listener.
	A good manager of behaviour.
	Counselling skills.
	Knowledge of disabilities.
	A person to whom others naturally turn.
PROCESS	Assessment (multi-professional); developing material for an individual transition plan (ITP).
	Preparing with others an ITP.
	Agreeing the ITP with the young person and the family.
	Facilitating the plan.
	Supporting the individual and the family.
	Monitoring the effectiveness of transition
ACTIVITIES	Providing information about further education, employment training, leisure/recreation, housing benefits, etc.
	Making relationships with the young person, families, teachers, social workers, employers/employees and agencies.
	Facilitating visits, interviews, placements and the young persons' contact with agencies.
	Providing continuity during transition.
	Communication and co-ordinating individual programmes.

Final Comment

This part of the report has summarised the views that emerged at the meeting of experts for the implications of a case management approach to transition to work for young people with disabilities. The emphasis has been to provide guidance to those who might wish to plan transitional arrangements for disabled youth.

The report shows that there are principles and practices capable of being translated, in appropriate forms, to other contexts. However, this requires a knowledge and understanding of the transition process. Effective transition will not be achieved where the departements, agencies and professionals who contribute to transition work in isolation one from another.

The experts meeting showed that there was general agreement, among those who had studied the problem, on the main characteristics of effective management. Issues of priority and emphasis can only be resolved in the context of the policies and practices in individual Member countries. It is to be hoped that this report will prove a useful basis on which to develop procedures for managing transition.

It is worthwhile repeating the main message again. Young people with disabilities need a continuity of support if they are to make a successful transition to adult life. It is crucial that departments, agencies and professionals work to agreed ends to provide this continuity so that independence in working life can be achieved by all.

WHERE TO OBTAIN OECD PUBLICATIONS – OÙ OBTENIR LES PUBLICATIONS DE L'OCDE

Argentina – Argentine
Carlos Hirsch S.R.L.
Galería Güemes, Florida 165, 4° Piso
1333 Buenos Aires   Tel. 30.7122, 331.1787 y 331.2391
Telegram: Hirsch–Baires
Telex: 21112 UAPE–AR. Ref. s/2901
Telefax:(1)331–1787

Australia – Australie
D.A. Book (Aust.) Pty. Ltd.
648 Whitehorse Road, P.O.B 163
Mitcham, Victoria 3132   Tel. (03)873.4411
Telex: AA37911 DA BOOK
Telefax: (03)873.5679

Austria – Autriche
OECD Publications and Information Centre
Schedestrasse 7
5300 Bonn 1 (Germany)   Tel. (0228)21.60.45
Telefax: (0228)26.11.04
Gerold & Co.
Graben 31
Wien I   Tel. (0222)533.50.14

Belgium – Belgique
Jean De Lannoy
Avenue du Roi 202
B–1060 Bruxelles   Tel. (02)538.51.69/538.08.41
Telex: 63220   Telefax: (02) 538.08.41

Canada
Renouf Publishing Company Ltd.
1294 Algoma Road
Ottawa, ON K1B 3W8   Tel. (613)741.4333
Telex: 053–4783   Telefax: (613)741.5439
Stores:
61 Sparks Street
Ottawa, ON K1P 5R1   Tel. (613)238.8985
211 Yonge Street
Toronto, ON M5B 1M4   Tel. (416)363.3171
Federal Publications
165 University Avenue
Toronto, ON M5H 3B8   Tel. (416)581.1552
Telefax: (416)581.1743
Les Publications Fédérales
1185 rue de l'Université
Montréal, PQ H3B 3A7   Tel.(514)954–1633
Les Éditions La Liberté Inc.
3020 Chemin Sainte-Foy
Sainte–Foy, PQ G1X 3V6   Tel. (418)658.3763
    Telefax: (418)658.3763

Denmark – Danemark
Munksgaard Export and Subscription Service
35, Norre Sogade, P.O. Box 2148
DK–1016 Kobenhavn K   Tel. (45 33)12.85.70
Telex: 19431 MUNKS DK   Telefax: (45 33)12.93.87

Finland – Finlande
Akateeminen Kirjakauppa
Keskuskatu 1, P.O. Box 128
00100 Helsinki   Tel. (358 0)12141
Telex: 125080   Telefax: (358 0)121.4441

France
OECD/OCDE
Mail Orders/Commandes par correspondance:
2 rue André–Pascal
75775 Paris Cedex 16   Tel. (1)45.24.82.00
Bookshop/Librairie:
33, rue Octave–Feuillet
75016 Paris   Tel. (1)45.24.81.67
    (1)45.24.81.81
Telex: 620 160 OCDE
Telefax: (33–1)45.24.85.00
Librairie de l'Université
12a, rue Nazareth
13090 Aix–en–Provence   Tel. 42.26.18.08

Germany – Allemagne
OECD Publications and Information Centre
Schedestrasse 7
5300 Bonn 1   Tel. (0228)21.60.45
Telefax: (0228)26.11.04

Greece – Grèce
Librairie Kauffmann
28 rue du Stade
105 64 Athens   Tel. 322.21.60
Telex: 218187 LIKA Gr

Hong Kong
Swindon Book Co. Ltd.
13 – 15 Lock Road
Kowloon, Hongkong   Tel. 366 80 31
Telex: 50 441 SWIN HX
Telefax: 739 49 75

Iceland – Islande
Mál Mog Menning
Laugavegi 18, Pósthólf 392
121 Reykjavik   Tel. 15199/24240

India – Inde
Oxford Book and Stationery Co.
Scindia House
New Delhi 110001   Tel. 331.5896/5308
Telex: 31 61990 AM IN
Telefax: (11)332.5993
17 Park Street
Calcutta 700016   Tel. 240832

Indonesia – Indonésie
Pdii–Lipi
P.O. Box 269/JKSMG/88
Jakarta 12790   Tel. 583467
Telex: 62 875

Ireland – Irlande
TDC Publishers – Library Suppliers
12 North Frederick Street
Dublin 1   Tel. 744835/749677
Telex: 33530 TDCP EI   Telefax : 748416

Italy – Italie
Libreria Commissionaria Sansoni
Via Benedetto Fortini, 120/10
Casella Post. 552
50125 Firenze   Tel. (055)645415
Telex: 570466   Telefax: (39.55)641257
Via Bartolini 29
20155 Milano   Tel. 365083
La diffusione delle pubblicazioni OCSE viene assicurata dalle
principali librerie ed anche da:
Editrice e Libreria Herder
Piazza Montecitorio 120
00186 Roma   Tel. 679.4628
Telex: NATEL I 621427
Libreria Hoepli
Via Hoepli 5
20121 Milano   Tel. 865446
Telex: 31.33.95   Telefax: (39.2)805.2886
Libreria Scientifica
Dott. Lucio de Biasio "Aeiou"
Via Meravigli 16
20123 Milano   Tel. 807679
Telex: 800175

Japan– Japon
OECD Publications and Information Centre
Landic Akasaka Building
2–3–4 Akasaka, Minato–ku
Tokyo 107   Tel. (81.3)3586.2016
Telefax: (81.3)3584.7929

Korea – Corée
Kyobo Book Centre Co. Ltd.
P.O. Box 1658, Kwang Hwa Moon
Seoul   Tel. (REP)730.78.91
Telefax: 735.0030

Malaysia/Singapore – Malaisie/Singapour
Co–operative Bookshop Ltd.
University of Malaya
P.O. Box 1127, Jalan Pantai Baru
59700 Kuala Lumpur
Malaysia   Tel. 756.5000/756.5425
Telefax: 757.3661
Information Publications Pte. Ltd.
Pei–Fu Industrial Building
24 New industrial Road No. 02–06
Singapore 1953   Tel. 283.1786/283.1798
Telefax: 284.8875

Netherlands – Pays–Bas
SDU Uitgeverij
Christoffel Plantijnstraat 2
Postbus 20014
2500 EA's–Gravenhage   Tel. (070 3)78.99.11
Voor bestellingen: Tel. (070 3)78.98.80
Telex: 32486 stdru   Telefax: (070 3)47.63.51

New Zealand – Nouvelle–Zélande
Government Printing Office
Customer Services
33 The Esplanade – P.O. Box 38–900
Petone, Wellington
Tel. (04) 685–555   Telefax: (04)685–333

Norway – Norvège
Narvesen Info Center – NIC
Bertrand Narvesens vei 2
P.O. Box 6125 Etterstad
0602 Oslo 6   Tel. (02)57.33.00
Telex: 79668 NIC N   Telefax: (02)68.19.01

Pakistan
Mirza Book Agency
65 Shahrah Quaid–E–Azam
Lahore 3   Tel. 66839
Telex: 44886 UBL PK. Attn: MIRZA BK

Portugal
Livraria Portugal
Rua do Carmo 70–74
Apart. 2681
1117 Lisboa Codex   Tel. 347.49.82/3/4/5
Telefax: 37 02 64

Singapore/Malaysia – Singapour/Malaisie
See "Malaysia/Singapore – "Voir "Malaisie/Singapour"

Spain – Espagne
Mundi–Prensa Libros S.A.
Castelló 37, Apartado 1223
Madrid 28001   Tel. (91) 431.33.99
Telex: 49370 MPLI   Telefax: 575 39 98
Libreria Internacional AEDOS
Consejo de Ciento 391
08009 –Barcelona   Tel. (93) 301–86–15
Telefax: (93) 317–01–41

Sweden – Suède
Fritzes Fackboksföretaget
Box 16356, S 103 27 STH
Regeringsgatan 12
DS Stockholm   Tel. (08)23.89.00
Telex: 12387 Telefax: (08)20.50.21
Subscription Agency/Abonnements:
Wennergren–Williams AB
Nordenflychtsvagen 74
Box 30004
104 25 Stockholm   Tel. (08)13.67.00
Telex: 19937 Telefax: (08)618.62.36

Switzerland – Suisse
OECD Publications and Information Centre
Schedestrasse 7
5300 Bonn 1 (Germany)   Tel. (0228)21.60.45
Telefax: (0228)26.11.04
Librairie Payot
6 rue Grenus
1211 Genève 11   Tel. (022)731.89.50
Telex: 28356
Subscription Agency – Service des Abonnements
4 place Pépinet – BP 3312
1002 Lausanne   Tel. (021)341.33.31
Telefax: (021)341.33.45
Maditec S.A.
Ch. des Palettes 4
1020 Renens/Lausanne   Tel. (021)635.08.65
Telefax: (021)635.07.80
United Nations Bookshop/Librairie des Nations–Unies
Palais des Nations
1211 Genève 10   Tel. (022)734.60.11 (ext. 48.72)
Telex: 289696 (Attn: Sales)
Telefax: (022)733.98.79

Taiwan – Formose
Good Faith Worldwide Int'l. Co. Ltd.
9th Floor, No. 118, Sec. 2
Chung Hsiao E. Road
Taipei   Tel. 391.7396/391.7397
Telefax: (02) 394.9176

Thailand – Thaïlande
Suksit Siam Co. Ltd.
1715 Rama IV Road, Samyan
Bangkok 5   Tel. 251.1630

Turkey – Turquie
Kültur Yayinlari Is–Türk Ltd. Sti.
Atatürk Bulvari No. 191/Kat. 21
Kavaklidere/Ankara   Tel. 25.07.60
Dolmabahce Cad. No. 29
Besiktas/Istanbul   Tel. 160.71.88
Telex: 43482B

United Kingdom – Royaume–Uni
HMSO
Gen. enquiries   Tel. (071) 873 0011
Postal orders only:
P.O. Box 276, London SW8 5DT
Personal Callers HMSO Bookshop
49 High Holborn, London WC1V 6HB
Telex: 297138 Telefax: 071 873 8463
Branches at: Belfast, Birmingham, Bristol, Edinburgh, Manchester

United States – États–Unis
OECD Publications and Information Centre
2001 L Street N.W., Suite 700
Washington, D.C. 20036–4095   Tel. (202)785.6323
Telefax: (202)785.0350

Venezuela
Libreria del Este
Avda F. Miranda 52, Aptdo. 60337
Edificio Galipán
Caracas 106   Tel. 951.1705/951.2307/951.1297
Telegram: Libreste Caracas

Yugoslavia – Yougoslavie
Jugoslovenska Knjiga
Knez Mihajlova 2, P.O. Box 36
Beograd   Tel. (011)621.992
Telex: 12466 jk bgd   Telefax: (011)625.970

Orders and inquiries from countries where Distributors have not yet been appointed should be sent to: OECD Publications Service, 2 rue André–Pascal, 75775 Paris Cedex 16, France.
Les commandes provenant de pays où l'OCDE n'a pas encore désigné de distributeur devraient être adressées à : OCDE, Service des Publications, 2 rue André–Pascal, 75775 Paris Cedex 16, France.

12/90

OECD PUBLICATIONS 2, rue André-Pascal 75775 PARIS CEDEX 16
PRINTED IN FRANCE
(96 91 01 1) ISBN 92-64-13448-4 - No. 45421 1991